CITY OF TORRANCE

75th Anniversary
1912 - 1987

AFTER THE BLACK DEATH

Interdisciplinary Studies in History
Harvey J. Graff, *General Editor*

AFTER THE BLACK DEATH

A Social History of Early
Modern Europe

GEORGE HUPPERT

INDIANA UNIVERSITY PRESS
BLOOMINGTON AND INDIANAPOLIS

Manufactured in the United States of America

Library of Congress Cataloging-in-Publication Data

Huppert, George, 1934–
After the black death

(Interdisciplinary studies in history)
Bibliography: p.
Includes index.
1. Social history—Modern, 1500–   2. Europe—
Social conditions. I. Title. II. Series.
HN13.H86 1986   306'.094   85-45580
ISBN 0-253-30446-6
ISBN 0-253-20404-6 (pbk.)

2 3 4 5 90 89 88 87

For Fernand Braudel

CONTENTS

PREFACE

This preface is an apology of sorts for all the things the author did not do. His aim was to write a short, readable book which might serve as an introduction to the social history of Western Europe in the period extending from the fourteenth to the eighteenth centuries. That is to say, from the time of the first outbreak of bubonic plague, in 1347, which was referred to as the Black Death by dazed survivors, to the time when the plague left Europeans alone. Its last threatening appearance, in the Mediterranean port city of Marseille, was observed in 1721.

The plague itself will not appear in this book. Those who witnessed the terrible epidemics thought of them as Acts of God, punishments meted out by the Almighty in retribution for some awful misdeed. Six centuries later, we are more likely to think that natural disasters are unrelated to human behavior. Epidemics, like hurricanes and tidal waves, we view as blind forces unleashed by natural causes—and nature's indifference to mankind we assume to be universal and unvarying.

Wind, rain, frost, or drought have crushed the hopes of farmers, quite impartially, in Spain as well as in the Ukraine, in Napoleon's reign as easily as in Nero's. Yet human beings are not always and everywhere equally helpless when confronted with natural disasters. In the fourteenth century, Europeans were especially vulnerable to disease because of a succession of famines from which they had suffered. Famines are not entirely natural disasters. They can be, at least in part, caused by imprudent behavior. There were too many mouths to feed in Western Europe, in the early fourteenth century.

After the Black Death had done its work, the survivors became more prudent. They did not allow themselves the luxury of multiplying again to the point of outstripping their resources as dramatically as they once had. To forestall famine, they learned to control population growth. They also developed techniques of long-distance trade and navigation which allowed the importation of grain from the thinly populated plains of Eastern Europe. Against epidemic diseases, they learned to enforce ruthless quarantines. In time, they learned to develop vaccines. They had been helpless against famine and disease, in the fourteenth century. By the eighteenth century, they had reached a remarkable level of resistance to both They had also enlarged their cities and transformed their political systems. They had invented guns, clocks, printed books, new kinds of ships, new forms of art and of religion, new philosophies, new sciences. They had discovered new continents and settled them. And they did all this before the French and Industrial revolutions were to accentuate the differences between Western Europe and the rest of the world even further.

One of the assumptions which governed the writing of this book is that historians have shown excessive concern for the French and Industrial revolutions. These momentous transformations of the political and economic realities of the western world exerted a deep, hypnotic power over historians, political economists, and journalists throughout the nineteenth century. One of the more lasting legacies from this epoch of fascination with the Declaration of the Rights of Man and with the arrival of the factory system has been a tendency to consider European society "feudal" and "traditional," right up to the summer of 1789.

In reaction against this approach to social history, some historians, more concerned with understanding the social changes that led to the late eighteenth-century revolutions than with absorbing their impact, advocate the minute examination of slow change over a long stretch of time, in a setting, of necessity, narrowly circumscribed: a single village over a period of a century, a single city in the course of a generation. The impetus for this approach we owe to scholars active on the eve of the First World War, among whom I should single out Professor Lucien Febvre, whose model study of the social life of a single province was published in 1912.[1] In that book, in subsequent ones, and in the pages of the journal *Annales*, which Febvre founded in 1929, in collaboration with the medievalist Marc Bloch, a new approach to social history gradually took shape. The influence of the *Annales* grew only slowly, and it was largely limited to French scholarship, at first. In the 1950s and '60s, however, the *Annales* approach was producing such tangible results that it began to serve as the acknowledged model for social historians in Italy, in England, in Germany, and in the United States. It is to this tradition of social history that the present book belongs.

It is a frequent misunderstanding of the *Annales* approach to assume that its practitioners are necessarily number-happy. For the study of historical demography, it is necessary, to be sure, to count births, marriages, and deaths. To determine economic trends, an accurate record of prices and wages is indispensable. The social structure of an urban community can hardly be grasped without an attempt at calculating the shifting percentages of rich, middling, and poor families, as they show up in the tax rolls. Acreage, crop yields, food consumption, cloth, and salt production—all these are appropriately grasped by statistical means.

But these are means only. The great merit of Lucien Febvre and of his most thoughtful collaborators has been that they never reduced social history to impersonal trends, never declared themselves satisfied with the mechanical recording of those things which happen to be calculable. Their ambition was to come as close to grasping the totality of historical experience as possible. Hence they chose to limit the scope of their inquiries to a manageable slice of terrain which was to be scrutinized, from the ground up, in every way.

The study of material civilization provides the foundation for an inquiry which should not stop short of examining family structure, social conflict, and religious beliefs. In the end, it becomes necessary, when following the proven methods pioneered by Febvre and Bloch, to enter, whenever possible, into the minds of individual men and women so as to understand their fears and hopes.

The specialized studies which I have consulted in the course of writing this book belong to this tradition of social history. They all suffer from the same, inevitable shortcoming; they are narrowly limited in scope. The chief difficulty experienced by the historian who attempts a synthetic description of Western European society is the difficulty of extracting, from a limited number of case studies, an overall understanding of rural and urban life for which one could claim some general validity. I do not claim to have overcome this difficulty. Not a single one of the generalizations attempted in the pages that follow is to be viewed as more than tentative. This is as it should be.

In order to contain the narrative within reasonable limits, I was forced to make choices, the most natural of which has been the choice of chronological limits. If there is one general conclusion that emanates forcefully from the specialized literature, it is the conclusion that there is, in the history of Western European society, a reasonably well-defined period of time during which something like a system of social relations comes into being, a system which may be contrasted with earlier and later developments, a system which was peculiar to Western Europe and which was, within Western Europe, fairly generally established, in spite of local variations. Among the distinguishing features of this system we will find a demographic pattern whose most obvious component is the voluntary limitation of births among the mass of the population by means of delayed marriage. The cautious marriage practices of western peasants and artisans, which have been understood only recently, are generally thought to have been conditioned by the catastrophes of the fourteenth century and the later recurrences of famine and disease which struck whenever the population reached a level of density incompatible with the fixed supplies of nourishment that could be drawn from the available land. Before the fourteenth century, there was still some room for population growth. After the eighteenth century, both the food supply and employment opportunities were to become more flexible, as a result of industrialization and global trade. It was only in the early modern period that a precarious balance between resources and consumption could not be upset without the gravest consequences. The density of settlement which had been reached in Western Europe by 1300 appears as the most fundamental trait of this society, governing its marriage practices, its family structures, its exceptional level of urbanization, its continued search for new markets and resources abroad, as well as the transformation of serfs into free men and of obedient subjects into quarrelsome rebels.

If the period of time under consideration may be defined as extending from the fourteenth to the eighteenth centuries, what of the territorial limits of Western Europe? On that question I have allowed myself some latitude. Instead of settling for a purely geographical border line, such as the Elbe River valley, I have, in effect, focused on the most densely populated and the most thoroughly urbanized regions: the Paris Basin, southeastern England, northern Italy, western Germany. One might almost say that "western" is used in this book as a social rather than a geographical expression, so that Italy appears more western by far than Portugal.

The choices I have alluded to thus far may create an impression of dutiful consistency on the author's part. This is an illusion. Far from trying to give each portion of Western Europe its due, as a textbook might—with separate chapters, say, on Scandinavia, the Danubian lands, and Flanders—I have made only feeble attempts to correct the imbalance which is the natural consequence of the history of historical scholarship. There is some deliberation behind my decision to use case studies, on occasion, which stake out exotic claims to an understanding of border areas such as the foothills of the Pyrénées, the Friuli region north of Venice, or the sierras of southern Spain. But the fact remains that the specialized literature is, at this writing, still dominated by French scholarship and that it is concerned with French data, primarily. Where recent monographs are available for regions other than France, they are not likely to be concerned with lands only marginally western: Florence, Genoa, Venice, Seville, Milan, Valladolid, Coventry, Frankfurt, Nürnberg, Nördlingen, Strassburg are among the cities represented in this newer literature. A glance at the reading suggestions in the back of the book tells the story. It is, of course, a partial story.

In sum, the social historian whose aim is synthesis cannot be expected to present a picture that is consistently thorough, since he is dependent on the specialized literature, which may be thinner for Norway or the Abruzzi than it is for Tuscany or Burgundy. But let us not jump to conclusions: poorly studied regions are not always the least densely settled or the most backward. No region in Western Europe ought to be of greater importance to the social historian than the Dutch provinces of the Netherlands in the sixteenth and seventeenth centuries. Yet there is not enough material available, so far, to grasp the social history of the Netherlands in this period, at least to my satisfaction.[2] Another surprising weakness is the absence of studies devoted to very large urban centers. There are no books about London, Paris, or Amsterdam, for instance, that could stand comparison with published studies of Beauvais, Coventry, or Nördlingen. It is simply more difficult to reconstruct the dynamics of a city of half a million inhabitants than it is to lay bare the social structure of a city of 10,000.

To the unevenness of the historical literature, add the unevenness of the author's education—and you have to conclude that a method must be devised for writing about Western European society in general, while sticking close to a limited number of case studies, each of them as representative as possible of broader patterns of behavior. This is the approach I have opted for—and I will be the first to confess to its limitations.

The advantages of this method, however, are also clear. Not the least of these is the opportunity to recreate, in considerable detail, the life of one village, of one city, of one family. This is a general book about European society which, at the same time, draws the reader, as concretely as possible, into real villages and real cities. The adoption of this narrative device has the advantage of reminding the reader of the fragility of generalization in history: Here is how things were in a village in the Sologne, in the seventeenth century; here is how social groups coexisted in a city in Picardy; this is what a revolt was like in Dauphiné, and here is how it went in Franconia; this is what an elderly miller, respected in his

village in the Friuli, thought about morality and mortality, in the sixteenth century; and this is how domestic slaves were treated in Tuscany, in
the fourteenth century. Throughout, I have worked hard at underlining
similarities, constants, and variations. But nowhere is the reader lured
into accepting as fact anything except the evidence of contemporary
documents, which may be interpreted in different ways. When he comes
to the end of this book, the reader ought to be saying: This has been an
introduction—the time has come to move on to the specialized literature.

ACKNOWLEDGMENTS

The writing of this book was made possible by the grant of a year's fellowship at the Institute for the Humanities, University of Illinois at Chicago.

AFTER THE BLACK DEATH

I

THE ETERNAL VILLAGE

Let us begin by looking at an ordinary European village in the seventeenth century. This village, Sennely, which has been carefully studied by Professor Bouchard, has a claim to being considered typical.[1] A population of some 500 to 700 persons is typical enough. The village's reliance on grain for bread-making as its chief crop is more than typical—it is universal. The thatch-roofed, windowless farmhouses, with their two rooms, attic, barn, and cowshed, are certainly normal.

Sennely is relatively isolated, as are most villages. Not that the city is far away; it is close enough so that tenant farmers pay their rents to absentee landlords in the city of Orléans. But the outside world does not impinge on the daily life of the villagers. Like most villages in preindustrial Europe, Sennely was a community of subsistence farmers whose needs were supplied locally: the rye grain, for bread; the cattle and pigs; the orchards that supply apples, pears, plums, and chestnuts; the garden vegetables; the fish in the ponds and the bees kept for honey and wax. Sennely had a miller, an innkeeper, a smith. There were part-time shopkeepers and weavers in residence. A villager hardly ever needed to go abroad.

This small, self-sufficient world is typical in another respect. It is fragile. The balance between resources and population is an uneasy one. The land is poor in Sennely. Water drains poorly. Evaporation from stagnant pools and ponds creates permanent ground fogs. This is not good land for growing grain. The poor soils of Sennely may not be typical. What is typical is the constraint under which the farmers operated, inasmuch as they had to grow grain, even though they would have been better off if they had concentrated on raising cattle.

What Sennely had in common with practically all European villages before the mid-nineteenth century was the need to be self-sufficient. Underdeveloped transportation and commercial networks forced the rural population to grow all essential crops, even those for which the land or the climate were unsuitable. Sennely could not buy grain and sell livestock in exchange. It was condemned to make do with its sandy soil. Unable to grow wheat, the preferred grain crop, Sennely planted rye. Poor yields were compensated for by the vast size of the village land, a good deal of it wasteland, swamps, and heath. It took about two hours to walk across the village's territory and half the farms were spread out at a considerable distance from the village center. This dispersed habitat, an adaptation to the poor soil, no doubt goes a long way toward explaining Sennely's lack of social cohesion. Although the village did possess a clear center, a street of houses, a square, a church, and a cemetery, most of the farms lay hidden in the distance, each of them screened by rows of oak trees.

Not surprisingly, travelers described the chief personality trait of the peasants of Sennely as suspicion. They seemed suspicious of outsiders and of each other and not much given to talking freely. Their physical appearance was remarked upon as distinctive. They tended to be stunted, bent over, and of a yellowish complexion. They were not born that way. The little children were said to be good looking, but by the time they had reached the age of ten or twelve, they assumed the generally unpleasant appearance of their elders. They did not look healthy. Their bellies were distended. They moved slowly, they had poor teeth, their growth was retarded. Girls reached the age of 18 before first menstruation.

What we have here, then, is a group of people living on the edge of deprivation. Malnutrition was normal in Sennely in the late seventeenth century. There are hints of better times in the past, but by the time the records become abundant enough for a clear analysis of this society, Sennely appears as a fragile entity, vulnerable to disease and, somehow, just barely, kept going in spite of the constant, threatening presence of death.

One third of the babies born died in their first year. Only a third of the children born in Sennely reached adulthood. Most couples had only one or two children before their marriage was broken up by the death of one parent. Women married late, at about age 23, on the average. Any given 100 women in Sennely would bear about 350 children in the course of their lives. Of these, only 145 would reach adulthood and marry in turn, 75 of them female. Allowing for 5 girls who would not marry, only 70 adult women were available to replace the 100 women of the preceding generation. Yet the population remained more or less constant. The villagers probably made up the deficit by marrying the daughters of transient artisans and laborers. When death struck a household, no time was wasted; widows and widowers remarried right away. Most first marriages occurred in the wake of a parent's death, so that the farm and the family could continue to function with a normal complement of hard-working men and women.

Fragile in the face of its poor harvests, constantly threatened by hunger and disease, Sennely just barely managed to reproduce itself, to hold on to life behind its hedges. Yet, for all that, Sennely was not badly off when compared to other villages. The peasants of the nearby Beauce plateau, a prime wheat-growing region, looked down with contempt on sullen, watery Sennely. But when harvests failed in the Beauce, there was nothing to fall back on, since all the land was plowed for wheat. A succession of bad harvests was enough to transform the peasants of the Beauce into starving beggars. Having put all their eggs in one basket, they were helpless when the wheat fields failed them. They took to the road, begging for food. And it is on such grim occasions, when the peasants of Sennely open their houses to starving vagrants and feed them generously, that we notice the hidden strength of Sennely's economy. Although it lives on the margin of poverty, Sennely never faces an all-out famine. Its inhabitants must have learned long ago that their meager grain crops had to be compensated for by making full use of the heath and ponds. They depended on their pigs, their cattle and sheep, their vegetables, fruit orchards, and fishing. It is this diversity, together with a low population density, that kept catastrophic famines away.

Not that everyone in Sennely enjoyed an equal level of protection against hard times. This was not a society of equals. The better-off farmers owned a team of horses and a plow. They did not exactly own their farms. They leased them from absentee landlords, but their custom-ary rights to the land were so ancient that they were not in danger of losing them. These leaseholders belonged to the European-wide category of rich peasants known as *laboureurs* in France and as *yeomen* in England. Their wealth, however, was entirely relative. Distinguished by their pos-session of the expensive team and plow, they nevertheless lived just this side of poverty. It is only when they are compared to less fortunate peasants that they appear rich.

The estates of the *laboureurs* of Sennely can be evaluated at somewhere in the 2,000 livres range. By comparison, the social category just below, that of the renters *(locataires)* who do not own horses and plows, was made up of families whose worth was only in the 600 livres range. These tenant farmers were constantly in danger of losing the land they rented and of being reduced to the level of hired hands. Hired hands *(journaliers)* in Sennely owned nothing except, perhaps, the roof over their heads, a garden, a pig.

There was another category of villagers, that of the artisans who lived in the village center and owned no land. Their level of fortune lay somewhere in between that of the renters and hired hands. About half the peasant families in Sennely belonged to the better-off categories of leaseholders and renters, who had some property. The other half of the village's population was made up of the families of hired hands and artisans who had no land at all.

A little to the side of these ordinary peasants, living on the main street of the village, their houses marked with painted signs indicative of their profession, we find three successful entrepreneurs: the smith, the miller, and the innkeeper. These families were among the most prosperous and influential in the village community. Barely involved in working the land, they dealt in goods and money. The innkeeper was also a contractor and a moneylender. There were horses and cows in his barn, his sheep grazed in the pastures, but he also bought up the grain owed to the Church and sold it on the open market. A handful of part-time shopkeepers of lesser wealth and stature completed the picture. They had a shop, a house, and a garden on the main street, but they could not live from trade alone. They also farmed and they dealt in cattle, hides, and wool.

On the fringes of village society, linked to it only in the sense that they owned property here, were rich outsiders who constituted the local élite. The priest, to begin with, whose house was the most imposing in the village. The priest had a comfortable income from rents and tithes assigned to the Church. He had a garden and an orchard. His house was a mansion of sorts, complete with salon, parlor, library, chapel, butler's room, stable, bakery, barn, and servants' quarters.

Side by side with the priest who presided over the Church's real estate interests in Sennely, there were three or four other outsiders, substantial men of property: a notary, a business agent, and an estate manager. They represented absentee landlords, but they also had property of their own. The estate manager had two farms which he leased out, rents from a number of tenants, and a large herd of sheep. He lived in a six-room house and he had a servant.

On the outer fringes of Sennely's territory, there were three small châteaux, belonging to wealthy gentlemen who were seen only occasionally, as they lived in the city and resided in their country châteaux only in summer or in the hunting season. The wealthiest of these gentlemen owned six farms locally, the others had three farms each.

Leaving the priest, the gentlemen, and their managers aside, we are still left with a village community marked by sharp contrasts of wealth and power. The landless peasants and artisans live in grim poverty. Their cottages are small, dark, and cold, they cannot afford firewood, they own only the clothes on their back and a pair of wooden clogs, their larders are often empty.

The more substantial farmers, meanwhile, are likely to possess reserves of bacon and cheese, wardrobes full of warm clothes, and much bedding to ward off the cold at night. In spite of these differences, there is no sign of strife in the village. This requires some explanation, especially since Sennely lacks most of the social controls one may find elsewhere. No resident lord provides leadership here, the priest's influence is thin. At most, he visits a family once in three years. As for family ties, they are too weak to provide cohesion.

Family relations, as revealed in the parish registers where births, marriages, and deaths are recorded, confirm the casual observer's view of the peasants of Sennely. Each family is on its own here. It is a bare-minimum family, consisting of a couple and one or two young children. For those who look back to the rural past with nostalgia, expecting to find large, noisy, heart-warming throngs of adults and children all living merrily under one roof, the evidence in Sennely is bound to prove a disappointment. These seventeenth-century peasant families are as isolated and as unstable as are modern families of wage earners living in impersonal housing projects on the periphery of industrial cities.

Grandparents are hard to find in Sennely, and so are aunts, uncles, or cousins living under one roof. The bread and bacon wrung out of each homestead cannot stretch to feed more than two adults and their babies. Bitter experience taught the peasants of Sennely to be calculating. They did not marry until death had cleared the way for the formation of a new family. Most young men and women waited until one of their parents had died before marrying and raising a new generation. As long as both parents were alive, the addition of another mouth to feed would have put a strain on the family's resources. As soon as one of the parents falls ill, however, the grown son or daughter must contemplate marriage to a partner who will replace the dying parent on the farm. There probably is not much sentiment involved in such matches. If the priest is to be believed, his parishioners marry only out of calculation. They do not worry about the bride's pretty face, they ask only how many sheep she will bring into the family. Sexual need probably does not influence the decision very much either, since promiscuity at an early age is a trademark of Sennely's young. Outsiders comment on this, some expressing shock. The boys and girls of Sennely, it seems, do not need to wait for marriage. They pet and kiss and fondle each other freely. Marriage, in this perspective, is business rather than pleasure.

The new family, founded in the shadow of death, is a partnership established for the purpose of continuing the timeless battle against hunger and solitude. It is not a very solid partnership. It will be broken up by the death of one of the partners within ten years or so. Just time enough to have a baby in the first year and several others, at two year intervals— four or five children in all. One or two of these will die of a contagious disease, aided by chronic malnutrition and unsanitary surroundings. When the mother herself dies, often in her early thirties, and usually from complications following childbirth, the widower is left with two or three orphaned children in his care. Almost instantly he finds a new wife. Half the recorded marriages in Sennely are second marriages of this kind. Should both parents fall victim to one of the recurring waves of murderous food shortages accompanied by illness, the children will be taken care of by the village. Orphaned children are not so much absorbed by relatives as by legal guardians appointed by the community. Unless the orphaned children are very young, they may not experience their parents' death as a profound dislocation, since it was the custom, anyway, especially among the landless families, to hand children over to more prosperous neighbors when they reached the age of seven or eight. They were old enough, by then, to become servants, apprentices, or shepherds. By the time they were 14, they were able to give a full day's work to their masters, so that caring for an orphaned child was not necessarily a losing proposition.

Few could afford the luxury of sentiment in Sennely. This was a society on a perpetual war footing, mobilized against the inroads of death, closing ranks in the aftermath of catastrophe. The men and women of Sennely were too much concerned with making a bare living and burying their dead, to lavish feelings on each other. Parents were not in a position to care for their children beyond their early years, nor were children prepared to come to the aid of destitute or sickly parents. Orphans were taken care of, not so much out of pity, but because they were human capital. A reasonably healthy orphaned girl, after serving some years as a kitchen maid in her guardians' household, could look forward to a marriage proposal from an older widower. Not Christian charity or family affection but labor shortages activated social welfare provisions.

Having observed how fragile family bonds seem to be in this village, we are naturally led to ask how the community functions when common action is called for. In what sense does one belong to Sennely? What are the sources of authority here, how are common standards of behavior agreed upon and enforced? To the extent that one can answer these questions one reaches the conviction that authority in Sennely does not have its source in kinship ties. There are no clans, no elders or patriarchs obeyed because of their position within a network of family relations. To the extent that there is a common identity in Sennely, it rests not on blood, birth, or lineage, but on artificial, man-made, deliberate solidarities.

All the families of Sennely, rich or poor, are members of the formal village community. This is a legal entity, capable of borrowing money and raising taxes. Its will is expressed by means of periodic assemblies. Major decisions are made by formal or informal polls of all the heads of household present. Although everyone has the right to speak at village meetings, in practice most assemblies are attended only by the more substantial taxpayers. The village assembly also manages and audits the financial affairs of the local church. It prevents disputes from arising, takes measures to protect the village against marauders, vagrants, and wolves, appoints shepherds for the common herd and a schoolmaster if the village can afford one.

The assembly's functions are important, but the villagers are more deeply, more emotionally involved in other formal organizations. Although the priest may not be important to the villagers, they view the church as theirs. They feel at home in this building their ancestors built and they maintain. The church and the adjoining cemetery constitute the heart of the community. From the priest's perspective, the peasants may appear indifferent to religion. Although they do come to hear mass on Sundays, both morning and afternoon, they refuse to come to confession. Neither penitence nor communion interest them. They are baptized at birth, they confess on their deathbed. This is the extent of their participation in the sacraments.

But they do come to church with pleasure. Unlike the village assemblies, which suffer from absenteeism, religious ceremonies bring out the whole village, rich and poor, men, women, and children. Sunday mass is a community event. Everyone is talking while the children chase each other in the aisles. Gossip is exchanged, business deals are made, young men and women eye each other. The peasants of Sennely come together at their church as often as possible, not only on Sundays but on Saturday afternoons too and on all possible holidays. Their social life revolves around the church, spills over into the village square in front of it, and fills the village inn.

Festivities of a private kind, the drinking and eating that punctuate family occasions such as christenings, weddings, and funerals, do keep the inn busy, but they are dwarfed by the banquets and parades organized by the religious brotherhoods. These are clubs, essentially male clubs, whose religious functions are not particularly well defined but whose social purpose is quite clear: the brotherhoods provide solidarities beyond the level of the family. Within a brotherhood, distinctions of wealth and status are forgotten. *Laboureur* and *journalier* sit side by side at the banquets and they march together in the parades of which there can be as many as 100 in a given year. The priest opposes these frequent festivities, but he has no choice in the matter. He is an outsider. His stay in the village is of limited duration. He cannot oppose traditions that are centuries old and much dearer to his parishioners than are the teachings of the Church. Not that the villagers were lacking in religious feeling. They had a particular devotion to the Virgin Mary and they offered up prayers to saints of whom they expected something in return. Their devotions were not quite orthodox in character. They venerated a particular saint as long as he proved effective in warding off illness and other disasters. If the saint failed to keep up his side of the bargain, they switched to another. The priest who lived in Sennely from 1676 to 1710—and whose diary is the source of much that we know about this village—did not care for the villagers' attitude toward religion. They used the church as a community hall, they showed little respect for the priest and little interest in the sacraments. Even though St. John was the official patron saint of Sennely, the villagers chose to pray to St. Sebastian instead. Presumably St. John had disappointed their expectations at some time in the past. While the priest Sauvageon was in residence, the villagers favored St. Sebastian who was reputed to be effective in curing illness. The most popular social organization in Sennely was the brotherhood of St. Sebastian, to which the villagers were willing to pay dues, although they contributed almost nothing to Sunday collections at church.

Religion played a large part in the lives of the peasants, but it was a religion of their own, designed to satisfy local needs. The priest Sauvageon was constantly irritated and frustrated. Had he wished to play a more active part in the village's religious life, he probably would not have been allowed to do so. His sense of appropriate piety and observances was too much at odds with local tradition. The difference between the priest's views and those of the villagers was not necessarily the difference between a rigorous and a lax interpretation of Church customs. During Lent, for instance, the villagers did fast. It is just that they went on fasting past the required number of days. They had their own unshakeable sense of what was right. Their favorite social and religious activities were the processions and banquets sponsored by the brotherhoods. The parades involved the whole village. The biggest of these was on Corpus Christi day, when the village street was covered with hay and straw, the church bells rang, and everyone came out dressed in his finery. The parade proceeded to the neighboring village. On this annual occasion, the public festivities served not only to unite the villagers of Sennely, but also to touch base with outsiders. When the procession reached the neighboring village, all the people of both communities attended mass together, after which they visited the cemetery. No religious procession was complete without the banquets and drinking bouts that wound up the big event as darkness fell.

Having spent some time observing a single village, we should now proceed to ask how representative Sennely may be of rural society in Western Europe. In the Kingdom of France alone, at the time when the records allow a reasonably close glimpse of Sennely, there were about 40,000 villages. In the regions of Western Europe as a whole—those, at least, that we are best informed about, including France, England, Spain, Italy, the Low Countries (modern Holland and Belgium), and parts of western Germany—we may be talking about something like 160,000 rural parishes. Each of these surely had its own character. Even so, we should be able to identify some fundamental traits common to most, if not all, of these communities. We will have to proceed cautiously, in later chapters, moving from the watery Sologne, where Sennely lies, to water-poor Hampshire, glancing at villages in the plains of Lorraine and in the high mountains of the Spanish sierras, including Mediterranean settings filled with permanent sunshine as well as Atlantic seashore villages drenched in rain and flavored by the smell of mussel beds and herring catches. Closing our eyes, momentarily, to sharp variations of soil, climate, language, and religion, we shall listen only to the constants, to the invariable realities that should make generalization possible.

As a starting point, I propose two categories that might serve to make sense of the mass of information we shall encounter. Let us call the first of these categories *constraints*, the second *autonomies*.

Approaching the scene from the vantage point of a North American or European society in the twentieth century, any seventeenth-century peasant community must give the impression of being hemmed in on all sides by brutal necessity. We see only the constraints in operation. The historian Gérard Bouchard indicates this in his choice of title: Sennely appears to him as an immobile village, where nothing changes and nothing can change. This may be an acceptable summation, not only for one village but for most, if we restrict our analysis to a few basic aspects of material life.

The population of Sennely does not grow. It cannot grow. If we examine the constraints which keep the population in check here, we will find that they are the very same constraints in effect everywhere else in Western Europe. The obstacle to population growth is an invisible barrier constructed out of the ratio between the land available for cultivation and the hunger of human beings.

This barrier was gradually erected over a period of some three hundred years. It was fully in place by the beginning of the fourteenth century. Before that time, no such constraint had existed. People had been scarce, unclaimed lands plentiful. Immense stretches of forest invited clearing. In this happy situation, the population had quadrupled in size, increasing most dramatically in those regions favored by fertile soil, a temperate climate, and easy access. In Christian Europe as a whole, there may have been as many as 65 million people making a living in the early fourteenth century. This was a high-water mark beyond which growth became impossible. This was especially the case in the most densely settled zones, the heartland of medieval Europe. Some 43 million people, out of a total of 65 million, lived in these favored regions which had been part of the Roman empire: Italy, France, the Low Countries, England, and western Germany. Within this preferred region there were clusters of particularly dense settlement in northern Italy, the Paris basin, and Flanders, where the ratio of people to land reached the level of 40, 50, even 80 to the square kilometer. Forests almost vanished. Churches were separated by no more than half an hour's walk from each other. This pattern of settlement, established by 1300, was not substantially altered before the eighteenth century.[2]

Throughout the four centuries we are concerned with in this book, European peasants lived in a straightjacket of their own making. They had multiplied freely and reached limits that could be breached only at the cost of the gravest perils. When vacant land suitable for homesteading was no longer to be had and every village's wheat fields and vineyards bordered upon another village's territory, the margin between survival and disaster narrowed dangerously. With too many mouths to feed and no further expansion possible beyond the customary limits of village lands, efforts were made to increase the grain crop within each village's boundaries. Timber was felled, swamps were drained, meadows were plowed under. Even poor stretches of gravelly soil and rock-strewn hillsides difficult for the plow to handle were requisitioned when the need for bread demanded desperate measures.

Such tactics merely delayed the inevitable catastrophe. Every one of these expedients was shown to be imprudent in the long run. With the forests gone, timber and firewood disappeared. Every acre of meadowland put under the plow reduced opportunities for grazing. Livestock herds shrank in size. Manure, essential for use as fertilizer, became scarce and the yields of the grain fields, already low in normal times, became even lower. Marginal land put under cultivation barely repaid the investment in seed. Unless new farming techniques could be introduced, to increase productivity, there was only one possible solution to the impasse—and that would have been to reduce the population. Increasing productivity proved impossible. Now the slightest frost, an invasion of locusts, a fever carrying off a few cows sufficed to upset the balance. Chronic malnutrition weakened resistance to disease. Small waves of famine and local epidemics prepared the way for the catastrophic epidemic of bubonic plague which broke out in the summer of 1347, racing northward from the Mediterranean faster than a forest fire. The Black Death, as it came to be known, destroyed perhaps as much as one third of the population within months.

For the survivors, land was plentiful again. Labor shortages were acute. Cattle went untended. Forests grew again. Several generations would be born, would reproduce, would die, before the murderous damages of 1347–48 were repaired. One hundred and fifty years later the population had not yet regained its medieval level. In the course of the sixteenth century, at last, the 60 million mark was passed and growth continued cautiously, shying away from dramatic increases. The pattern set in the fourteenth century was to remain in effect. Population could grow only so much without inviting famine and disease. The most fundamental constraint was now securely in place.

In some measure, the brakes were applied by impersonal forces: viruses, bacteria, rodents, insects, bad weather, the ravages of war. The plague remained endemic until 1721. Other diseases took their threatening turn: syphilis, smallpox, typhus, influenza. But there never was a catastrophe again to approach the scale of the holocaust of 1347. Famine, the great scourge, continued to hover near enough, inspiring fear, a wolf at the door baring its teeth in the dead season. But famines became less threatening in time. After 1700, its pressures became less frequent, less severe, pushed back into pockets of badlands. One cannot escape the suspicion that Europeans had learned to live within the constraints imposed by inflexible harvests. The evidence in Sennely and elsewhere confirms this suspicion.

Sennely, even though cursed with poor grain lands, managed to avoid major famines and epidemics. How? By keeping a low profile, by making sure that its population was not allowed to exceed its resources. The number of families making a living within the confines of Sennely's territory was not subject to variation. The land could support only about 50 farms. These farms could not be subdivided. Each of them constituted a balanced portfolio of securities, of separate lines of defense: grain, vegetables, orchards, grazing, ponds. Some properties were more profitable than others, but none was abundant enough to overcome the peasants' caution: the farms had to be kept whole. Any diminution of these units of production was an invitation to catastrophe.

Having more than two or three children would upset the balance. Each generation's goal was to replace itself without adding to the number of mouths to feed. This goal was achieved by delaying marriage until there was room on the farm for a new couple and their eventual children. The death of a parent activated the son's or daughter's marriage. If the new couple proved too fertile, if Fate showed too much kindness to their infant children, so that more than two or three survived infancy, then the parents might well arrange to hire the surplus children out to more prosperous farmers who could use extra help. The larger farms could feed more people than the bare minimum of two adults and two children. It was only because of these larger farms that Sennely could support the landless half of its population, the hired hands, the servant girls, the shepherds who worked for little more than their daily bread.

What we are looking at is an artfully balanced social organization. The men and women of Sennely understood and accepted the limits of their resources and learned to live within these limits. Long ago, when land was plentiful and people scarce, there had been no need for such cautious ways. No doubt the girls had married earlier then and families had been larger. But since the fourteenth century, grim lessons had been learned. Sennely had accepted the new way of dealing with scarcity. Like all the other peasant communities in Western Europe—at least those whose records have been studied so far—Sennely had declared its independence from worldwide, instinctive patterns of behavior. Instead of bearing children as soon as they were nubile, the girls of Sennely accepted the constraint imposed by need. They delayed marriage and childbearing for as long as might be necessary to insure their future children's subsistence. For some girls that time might never come. They were prepared to conceive only when an offer of marriage was made. Such offers were contingent upon the inheritance of the family land.

Delayed marriage may have been the most important element within the social system created by European peasants after the fourteenth century. It is, in any case, the most readily identifiable one. By delaying marriage, European peasants set a course that separated them from the rest of the world's inhabitants. As early as 1377, in a very large sample from England, the trend is visible. Of all the girls over the age of 14—and therefore presumably capable of conceiving—only 67 percent were married and bearing children. That proportion would be down to 55 percent in the seventeenth century. Outside of Western Europe, so far as such calculations can be made, the proportion of nubile girls who actually married and conceived would be close to 90 percent.[3] A rough summation of the discoveries made by historical demographers would be to say that European peasants adapted to scarce resources by limiting potential births by as much as 50 percent through unnaturally late marriage and conception. In so doing they bowed to constraints, but they also achieved a degree of autonomy.

II

THE FREEDOM
OF THE CITY

"It is a commonwealth of men who live
magically outside of Nature's order."[1]

No sharper contrast can be imagined than that which greeted travelers after a day's march through the countryside: When the high stone ramparts of the city became visible in the distance, a new world beckoned, a world so different from the rural society stretched out below as to invite astonishment and wonder. Pilgrims, soldiers, beggers, and other victims of the implacable constraints that governed rural life, displaced persons whom the land could not feed, all must have gawked at the sight of urban wealth and power. Coming from villages which could support only a fixed population of a few hundred people, they could not help but marvel at the miracle performed in front of their eyes. Behind those enormous walls, built of expensive quarry stone, lived 10,000, 20,000, even 30,000 people who ate and dressed sumptuously without plowing or herding.

When he was allowed to pass through the heavy gates, the peasant saw fine white bread piled high in the baker's shops, delicate bread, rich man's bread, long loaves, round loaves, buns and sweetened rolls with shining glazes, honey cakes, and pies filled with meat or fruit. Down the street, suckling pigs and capons could be seen roasting on spits and wine shops and ale houses beyond counting graced the city's neighborhoods, a picture of abundance imaginable to countryfolk only at annual harvest feasts. In the city, Nature's haphazard order seemed transformed and regulated, allowing steady abundance, year-round luxury.

Lest we think that the peasants' vision of the city's wealth was an illusion, a mirage akin to those that befall thirsty desert travelers in the noonday heat, let us turn to the well-kept archives of some representative cities. Take the Spanish city of Valladolid, for instance, a city of some

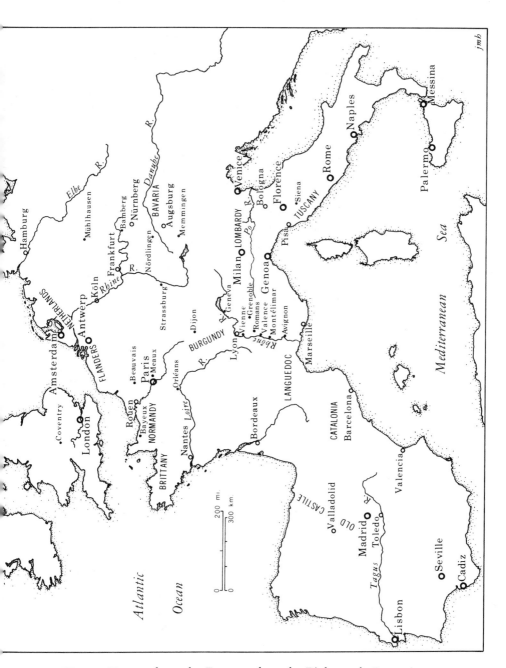

Western Europe from the Fourteenth to the Eighteenth Centuries
John Hollingsworth

30,000 inhabitants situated at the confluence of two rivers in the plain of Old Castile. Working from sales tax records and other sources from the sixteenth century, Bartolomé Bennassar estimates that enough grain entered Valladolid to provide something like 234 liters per inhabitant annually, which is plenty. Beef, almost entirely absent from the peasants' diet, was for sale in the butcher shops of Valladolid. Its consumption reached about 50 pounds per person annually. Several liters of olive oil and a staggering amount of wine—more than 100 liters per person—were sold each year within the city. More meat was eaten by the citizens of Valladolid in the sixteenth century than by the average Spaniard today. Adding up the caloric intake in the city as a whole, counting only bread, meat, fish, oil, and wine, Bennassar comes up with an estimate of 1,580 calories a day per inhabitant. This is a minimum estimate. When items of common consumption not easily traced in the tax records, such as sausages, chickens, eggs, cheese, honey, vegetables, and fruit are added, the peasants' suspicion is largely confirmed: City people were well fed, even though they grew no food. Above all, their supplies never stopped flowing in. How could that be?

The peasant who came to town to pay his rent no doubt had a ready answer to this question: City people were parasites who lived off the peasantry. Peasants ate black bread so that they could pay their rents, tithes, and taxes with cartloads of fine wheat. They flavored their soup with skimmed milk, while the cream was sent to town. Lambs and calves were driven to the city's slaughterhouses, rural vineyards and precious timber belonged to city people. As winter set in and the days became shorter, the villagers prepared for cold and hunger. Having given up about one third of their harvest to landlords, priests, and tax collectors, they could only hope that there would be enough left to keep them alive until summer came again.[2] Shortages spelled starvation for them, with no hope of rescue.

The city, meanwhile, stocked up. Within sight of the ramparts, huge barns belonging to bishops and abbots filled up with the tithe grain seized from the peasants' fields. Within the city, attics and cellars were packed with a year's supply of grain, wine, oil, salt pork, and other essentials.[3]

On the face of it, the peasants' view of the city as a devouring monster in the midst of a subjected countryside would not seem far off the mark. A bitter truth, it would seem, sufficient, on occasion, as an incitement to riot and rebellion. Sufficient, also, to inspire caution in the city, whose ramparts were guarded day and night. The gates were locked at sundown, vagrants were driven out, curfew was enforced. Anyone who approached the city with other than peaceful intentions could not fail to reflect on the high cost of crime. Over the entrance gates, impaled on iron stakes, one could see the severed, bloody, eyeless heads of executed criminals.[4] Even minor theft, a loaf of bread grabbed from a market stall, brought on swift and severe punishment.[5] The well-fed, softly robed proprietors, the *popolo grasso,* the *ricos hombres,* knew how to guard their wealth.

Can urban wealth really be accounted for by rural poverty? Only in part. It is an explanation that holds true only as long as we are talking about a self-sufficient, local, closed economy. A small market town with a population of two or three thousand, with no significant industry and little long-distance trade, may consume a disproportionate share of the district's finite agricultural production. Such small towns, however, are not real cities. They are semirural. The difference between their economy and that of purely rural communities is a difference in degree only, the difference between small fish and even smaller ones. Some of the wealth drained from the countryside finds its way into such market towns, but most of it is channeled toward larger cities. Small towns are weak magnets, capable of attracting and holding only small filings. The bulk of the traffic in grain, cattle, hides, wool, wine, taxes, and tithes heads, inexorably, toward the larger predators who can be found only in true cities.[6] The village priest is able to keep only a fraction of the tithe income, the small-town church does better, but the final destination of ecclesiastical revenues is in the bishops' palaces and in the business offices of large monasteries. Royal taxes travel in the same way. Some profit sticks to middlemen, but the lion's share goes to bankers, financiers, and treasury officials in major cities. As for landowners, they have their hierarchy also. The important ones are found in important cities.

When we turn to such cities, we find that they are not simply magnets attracting the surplus produced by the rural population. A city with 10,000 inhabitants could, just conceivably, be fed in large part with the grain of the surrounding countryside—the *tierra, contado,* or *plat pays* subject to the city's rule. A dozen villages within a radius of 15 or 20 kilometers from the ramparts could almost always be treated as the city's own. But a city of 20,000 could not live on the production of its *tierra.* Cities with a population of 100,000 required provisions to be brought in from the ends of the known world—and such cities housed about one fourth of the total urban population.

A city controlled its own *tierra,* through landownership, share cropping, and legal jurisdiction. At the confines of its *tierra,* however, the city's jurisdiction would come up against that of neighboring and rival cities. Large cities could not possibly be supplied from local resources alone. And yet they not only managed to acquire food, they acquired it lavishly and steadily. Urban markets, where cheap grain and meat were to be found in large quantities throughout the year, no doubt struck peasants as awesome spectacles, fairy-tale devices like those magic tablecloths whose lucky owners need only issue a command to find the table set.

In a sense, city people did live outside of Nature's order. They fed themselves not by cultivating land, but by cultivating money. Money knows no seasons. It is immune to frost, safe from locusts, and it comes, when properly tended, in quantities that may seem unlimited. Money, alas, does not grow on trees. It could not flourish within the subsistence economy of preindustrial villages. For proper growth, it required almost unimaginably complex circumstances, including massive consumption, industry, credit, and transportation. These requirements were met by medieval cities so successfully that few significant refinements were added after the fourteenth century.

Thirty thousand wage-earning consumers within the walls, there you have the first element of an economy that will float free of the constraints gripping the peasant world. Ten thousand suffice to tip the balance. One hundred thousand transform the rules of the game beyond recognition. Temper those figures as much as you like. Remind us of the fact that many urban families own plots of land just outside the walls which they cultivate for their own needs. Think of the rich who own large farms in the *tierra*. Think of the poor whose purchasing power is so weak that four fifths of their income is spent on bread alone. With all this in mind, it remains true that the city represents a large mass of consumers who pay cash for their daily needs. This fundamental distinction separates the urban economy from the rural world.

In and of itself, the concentration in cities of large numbers of men and women dependent on distant food-producing regions could well have been disastrous: One need only think of the bloated, helpless conurbations in modern Africa and Asia, filled with destitute and unemployable peasants. The European city, however, was different from its Asian and African counterparts in fundamental ways. Even the cities of the Roman Empire bore little resemblance to the medieval cities which were to grow up on the same sites a thousand years later. Roman garrison cities became, in time, the headquarters of medieval bishops. Monasteries were erected nearby. Feudal barons held court within the safety of the earliest fortifications. Merchants and craftsmen came to supply the needs of the new potentates. It was in the eleventh and twelfth centuries that

European cities began to veer away from the traditional functions associated until then with urban life. They ceased to be military and administrative headquarters only, subject to the capricious wants of warlords. The turning point was reached with the creation of the commune, a voluntary association of merchants and artisans sworn to mutual aid who elected their own leaders and seized power from lords and bishops. A chronicler's account of such a coup d'état in the French city of Laon, in the year 1122, may serve as a summary illustration of almost identical events elsewhere: "When the bishop was collecting money after the noon offices, suddenly there arose throughout the city the tumult of men shouting 'commune'. Then, through the cathedral, a crowd of bourgeois attacked the bishop's palace with swords and lances. The nobles rallied to the bishop, having sworn to give him aid against such an assault if it should occur."[7]

The communal form of political organization owed little to the past, although medieval bourgeois were inclined to imagine ancient Roman antecedents for their polity. They called their leaders consuls, their flags and seals bore ancient imagery, their poets indulged in fanciful comparisons. But the bourgeois owed nothing to popes, to emperors, to princes. They declared their towns to be sovereign communities. They declared themselves free men. They owed allegiance, they claimed, only to distant kings or emperors, a purely theoretical allegiance, since it could not be enforced. They bribed royal treasuries to purchase elaborate charters that specified their liberties. And they built formidable ramparts, bastions, moats, and towers to protect the commune against its enemies.[8]

The emancipation of the cities and their spectacular growth occurred at a time of general prosperity. The countryside was filling up with farms, land prices rose, the population density, in some cases, reached levels it would not surpass until the twentieth century. The cities kept bulging at the seams, employing large numbers of masons and laborers to expand the circumference of the walls. In the growth period of the late twelfth century, Bologna, for instance, pushed its city limits from a nucleus covering fewer than 50 acres to include an area of about 250. Florence came close to reaching similar dimensions, Pisa stretched even farther, and Milan soon covered some 500 acres.[9]

By the end of the thirteenth century, Christian Europe, from the Atlantic coasts to the Danube borderlands and from the Baltic to the Mediterranean shores, was full to the brim, with villages bordering upon villages and walled cities sitting in the midst of their *tierras* in such numbers that one may speak of an unprecedented development in the history of the human species. Over a total area of some 2.5 million square kilometers, a mass of 60 or 70 million people lived side by side, leaving few lands vacant and constituting an uninterrupted blanket of fields and houses, with some 130,000 churches built in such proximity to each other that anyone climbing to the top of the steeple of his parish church was likely to see five or six other steeples on the horizon. Large concentrations of human beings had been seen before, but probably never such a mass of continuous settlement.[10]

Even though epidemics cut the population down in the fourteenth century, the network of fields, villages, and cities remained in place. By the early sixteenth century, Europe had recovered. The cities were filling up once again, spilling over beyond their walls, extending into newly built suburbs. Giants like Naples and Paris were passing the 200,000 mark. Venice, Milan, Genoa, Florence hovered at the 100,000 level, soon to be joined by Lisbon, Rome, Palermo, Messina, Seville, Madrid, London, Antwerp, and Amsterdam. If a fourth of the urban population was concentrated in these giant metropolitan centers, the equivalents of our New York and Tokyo, a larger proportion by far lived in innumerable cities of medium size, more or less in a class with Valladolid, in the 10,000 to 40,000 range. Many of these were clustered in the older zones of dense settlement, in Italy or Flanders. Others sat on major trade routes, at the mouth of large rivers, on the seacoasts: Marseille, Lyon, Bordeaux, Nantes, Rouen, Hamburg, Danzig, Augsburg, Köln, Lübeck, Nürnberg, Magdeburg, Strassburg, Barcelona, Valencia, Cadiz. These old cities retained their communal organization, their strong walls, their rich *tierras*, and the commercial and industrial capacities that were the secret of their independence.

As we come closer to defining these cities, we are bound to abandon mere numbers as a suitable method of description. Thirty thousand people may constitute a city in a census taker's mind.[11] The historian has gotten nowhere if he accepts such a definition, which explains nothing. Thirty thousand people crowded together in narrow streets could be soldiers, courtiers, campfollowers, beggars, monks, and slaves dependent on the largesse of a warlord. Such concentrations are familiar to historians of preindustrial Japan or Russia.[12] In sixteenth-century Europe, only Papal Rome came close to resembling such parasitical centers dependent on a princely court.[13]

Perhaps the surest way of understanding European cities as they were before the nineteenth century might be reached by setting aside census records and by forgetting, for the moment, the fortifications and houses, even though information about them fills the archives. The existence of such records is in itself remarkable, to be sure. Nowhere else in the world can historians count on finding public and private papers concerning property, inheritance, taxation, and municipal expenditures in such profusion. Even detailed minutes of city council meetings going back to the fourteenth century have been preserved in the well-kept archives of European communes. Astonishing though this feat of conservation may be, the very profusion of documents concerning property and real estate can have the effect of luring historians away from other, more difficult, questions. It is useful to know that the walls surrounding Nürnberg had a circumference of 17,000 feet, that the inner ring of fortifications was buttressed with 83 towers spaced 150 feet apart, while the outer ring counted 40 towers and was surrounded by a trench 100 feet wide throughout. It is even better to have a census of 1561 for Valladolid which records the existence of precisely 6,572 houses.[14] But too free a fascination with real estate may lead us into an anachronistic view of what these cities were all about. We run the risk of missing the heart of the matter, which is that cities were only accessorily constituted of stones, bricks, tiles, timber, thatch, and slate. In their minds, the bourgeois were more than simply residents of a town: they were members of a commune.

The distinction becomes clear when we come to realize that there were men and women residing in every city who were not members of the commune, who were excluded from membership. Among the more obvious categories of people who may have been allowed to reside in the city although they were excluded from membership in the commune, we must count the poor and the foreign, two categories defined rather broadly by contemporaries.

The poor, those who could not pay taxes, those who had no regular employment or domicile, made up a significant proportion of any city's population.[15] The foreign included not only foreigners in the modern sense—subjects of another prince—but all those who came from beyond the walls, even if they were natives of a town no more than an hour's walk away, even if they had been born and raised in a village of the city's own *tierra,* within sight of the city's church spires. Such foreigners could, in time, become citizens of the commune if they could meet certain requirements. A residence requirement, to begin with, which could vary from one year to ten. A financial requirement, also, including the payment of a onetime fee at the time of joining the commune and proof of solvency, the ownership of a house or proof of payment of a specified minimum in rent.[16] Neither residence nor financial contributions sufficed to achieve citizenship. It was also necessary to join the religious community, to become a member of a given city parish. In this way Protestants could be excluded from citizenship in Catholic cities, Catholics in Protestant ones, and Jews everywhere. Needless to say, servants who, by definition, were dependents living in their master's household, were excluded from the rights of citizenship. But so were noblemen, in many instances, unless they removed themselves from castles and courts and took up permanent residence within the walls, fulfilling the duties expected of bourgeois. Priests and monks were not citizens either, since they would not acquit themselves of the obligations of citizenship: they paid no taxes, bore no arms, swore no oath to the commune. Their status was ambiguous, since they could be considered aliens by virtue of their subjection to the Pope. This list of marginal residents is not exhaustive. The presence of slaves in a number of Mediterranean cities is worth mentioning, the marginal rights of sailors in Atlantic seaports, of oarsmen in Mediterranean ports is worth remembering, the dreaded presence of soldiers who were not fully answerable to the commune can hardly be forgotten, and most noticeable of all, there were the vagrants, beggars, and outlaws who streamed into large cities, especially in times of war and famine. There were traveling journeymen as well, who stayed in hostels, taverns, and rented rooms; there were pilgrims, mule drivers, barge men, traveling troupes of actors and acrobats, peddlers, students, mendicant friars. All these categories of people, distinguished by different styles of dress, speaking different dialects and languages, were to be found in the city, though they were not members of the commune.

The local poor alone could make up as much as 10 percent of the population. Servants may well have accounted for another 20 percent.[17] We are really in the presence of two distinct conceptions of the city. The narrow view includes only the sworn members of the commune, the *universitas* of native householders whose names were listed in the tax rolls. Let us use the term *bourgeois* to describe them and let us call the rest inhabitants. This use of the French word *bourgeois* is a little arbitrary, since its meaning was to change in time. It was close to meaning "full members of the commune" in the fifteenth century. By the eighteenth century, it was often used more narrowly to refer only to the more honorable and prosperous segment of the citizenry, becoming almost synonymous with "people of property." We shall use it in the older sense here.

The city of the bourgeois was a carefully regulated community, original in conception, sharply distinct from what we call cities elsewhere in the world and at other times. Twelfth-century Europeans may not have realized how different their cities were from those of the ancient world. But they did not fail to observe the contrast between their communes and the feudal society beyond the walls. Nor did feudal knights look kindly upon the bourgeois. They were dumbfounded by the city's wealth. What struck them even more deeply was the arrogance of the bourgeois who did not defer to noblemen.

"They sit side by side, a meeting of neighbors, the mayor and his aldermen and other bourgeois, so many of them," observes a character in a twelfth-century dramatic poem. The knight observes the town crier calling out, the people assembling, the bells of the commune ringing to warn against danger. "There is not one of these villeins who does not come forward armed with his pitchfork." Angered by the lack of respect shown toward his lordship, the knight's lady companion cries out: "Ho! Ho! What a bunch of villeins, enraged dogs, band of dirty serfs."[18]

But serfs they were not. Coming from a rural world still, in the twelfth century, divided into serfs and lords, a knight would not know what to do with this new species, these bourgeois who did not fit into the feudal scheme. They were not knights, they were not priests. Were they villeins then, "dirty serfs" who belonged to some lord? But what kinds of serfs would these be, who did not till the land and sat in the shadow of their bell tower, sleek and fat, dressed in fine cloth—and unimpressed by their natural superiors?

From an aristocratic perspective, the bourgeois appear unnaturally wealthy and unnaturally rebellious. If rural society is taken as the standard, these contentions are true enough. Where agriculture is the only natural source of wealth, the wealth of the city may be deemed unnatural. Where authority is thought to proceed naturally only from above, from counts and dukes whose right to rule is hereditary and sanctioned by kings, by popes, by God Himself—there the bourgeois must appear as rebellious subjects. Seen from within, however, the city was an orderly community, however mysterious it might appear to peasants, knights, or priests. The wealth of cities was the result of hard work and urban power rested on explicit principles of authority.

Medieval cities owed both their wealth and their independence to industry. The production of cloth, of guns, of ships—and of hundreds of other specialized goods that made each city's fame—was intricately linked to the commune's political organization and to a system of exchanges that was to assume global proportions. To the outsider, the bourgeois commune might have appeared as a walled oasis, an alien presence in a world of fields, shutting out the powers of the rural world, denying the authority of lords, devouring the substance of the peasants. A traveler familiar with the workings of the city would see nothing of the sort. He would observe fleets of barges moving downstream, loaded with grain, timber, hay, and salt. Shiploads of raw wool, of wood, of hops, iron, marble, and limestone were unloaded at the docks. Herds of cattle, sheep, and horses were driven overland from faraway pastures and feedlots. Bolts of finished cloth were sent out toward distant markets, armor, guns, nails, rope, barrels of wine, fine silk cloth, polished fixtures made of steel, bronze, or brass, enameled pottery, saddles, shoes, plowshares, leather bags filled with silver and gold coins. As he approached, the traveler would find himself jostled along the narrow road. Slowed down by traffic jams, caught up in slow-moving convoys of mule-drawn carts, pushed aside by galloping dispatch riders carrying mail and valuables, he would have time to notice the water mills positioned along the riverbank, their wooden wheels churning to power the grindstones of millers and the hammers of fullers. Narrow streams and man-made canals would attract his attention, as they were filled with industrial waste.

There is no need to single out urban giants like Paris. Or to dwell on booming cities like Madrid, whose tentacular reach drew in supplies on a Gargantuan scale: 50,000 sheep, 60,000 horses, 12,000 oxen, 10,000 calves, 13,000 pigs, every year.[19] Any medium-sized city in Western Europe was bound to appear to the approaching traveler as a kind of pumping station, drawing in food and raw materials and spewing out finished goods.

Whether they made goods and sold them, whether they were tailors or money changers, the bourgeois of any late-medieval city were members of craft fellowships. The commune was the association of all the crafts. The power of the commune was exercised by an elected city council and the right to vote was limited not only to tax-paying native residents, but usually restricted, as well, to those who held membership in a craft. In this way, not only the poor and the foreign were excluded from participation in political rights, but also those who did not work in a recognized trade. The commune was the creation and the preserve of the working population, it being understood that some kinds of work were especially important to the city and that senior masters and prominent merchants carried more weight than did ordinary artisans and shopkeepers.

A good case study of a middling sort of city is provided by Pierre Goubert's analysis of Beauvais in the seventeenth century.[20] Beauvais was quite ordinary in most respects. Located 76 kilometers to the northwest of Paris and 80 kilometers to the northeast of the great seaport of Rouen, Beauvais remained relatively isolated, especially since the little river that ran through it was not navigable. The original nucleus of the city occupied some 25 acres of ground surrounded by swamps and marshes. Roman engineers drained the wetlands. After the barbarian invasions of the third century, the city was walled and the river was re-routed so as to provide a moat at the foot of the ramparts. On this original Roman site, the medieval cathedral was built. In the period of expansion, between the tenth and thirteenth centuries, the city grew tenfold. The medieval walls enclosed about 250 acres and continued to serve in the seventeenth century.

Pierre Goubert describes the impression Beauvais made on travelers who came down from the heights above the city. Seeming to sink in a sea of vineyards, the old city lay at the bottom of a marshy depression, encircled by ramparts and moats, the river dotted with water mills and soiled by the by-products of the wool and dye industries. Within the walls, the city was a jumble of thatch and tile roofs, dominated by 20 slate-covered steeples and the massive, unfinished cathedral which stood out above everything else.

The population of Beauvais remained steady at about 13,000 for centuries. Supplied with grain, cattle, and wool by the surrounding countryside, the city paid for its bread and meat with its earnings in the international cloth market. Beauvais produced both woolens and linens. Almost half the inhabitants made a living directly from textiles. The great cloth merchants of Beauvais sent their bolts of fine cloth to Lyon, Geneva, London, Lisbon, and Cadiz. The rural hinterland fed the city, but it was not a suitable market for its finished products. Fine woolens were expensive. They did not penetrate the closed economy of the villages. The wool from local sheep was spun and woven for regional consumption, but the high-priced cloth for export depended on high-quality wool imported from England or Flanders at one time and, later, from French provinces south of the Loire and even from Spain. In this way the city's economy slipped away from the simple economy of the villages. The main business of Beauvais was cloth and the earnings of the cloth trade depended on markets as far away as Central Europe, the Mediterranean regions, and, eventually, even the Americas.

The social and political life of the city was closely connected with production for export. Organized as a commune since 1099, Beauvais was ruled by an elected city council. Voting rights were limited to the masters of the crafts. The crafts of the cloth trade naturally exerted more power than those associated with local consumption. Within the cloth trade, power rested with the wholesale merchants who sent their wares to Paris, Rouen, or Lyon and imported raw wool from as far away as Spain. It was from within this small group, this bourgeois oligarchy, that aldermen and mayors were usually chosen.

In this respect Beauvais was typical. Most cities in Western Europe were governed by a small group of wealthy merchants, even though the trappings of communal democracy remained in place. As soon as a city's trade had liberated it from the constraints of a purely local economy, it was pushed into a new world of European-wide dependence. Beauvais could not meet demand without the wool shipped from Burgos and Orléans. Hence the fate of the city was in the hands of the greater merchants, those who had the capital reserves and the business connections that could provide employment for the weavers and dyers of Beauvais.

Although the masters of the textile crafts ran their own workshops, they were dependent on the wholesale merchants who sold them wool and who bought up their entire production of finished cloth. Pierre Goubert illustrates the dependence of the masters by introducing his readers into a Beauvais wool workshop. The year is 1685 and the occasion is the death of the master's wife, which necessitates an inventory of the estate. Master Charles Toupet is not badly off. He employs 12 workers. As long as orders keep coming and his five looms are kept busy, he earns enough to feed his family. But he is entirely dependent on three merchants who buy the cloth produced in his shop. He cannot sell the cloth locally. He obtains his raw materials on credit. In spite of the size of his enterprise, he has very little property of his own. The workshop and the family apartment above it are rented premises. Should demand for Beauvais cloth diminish in Montpellier or in Geneva, Toupet will have to let his workers go. They will join the ranks of the unemployed—and Toupet will not be far behind. The local shopkeepers who depend on the custom of Toupet's family and employees are also, in the last resort, dependent on the merchants who order Toupet's cloth.

Close to 1,000 households—perhaps 4,000 people in all—were directly involved in textile production in Beauvais. Another 582 households— some 2,000 persons—catered to local needs. This includes the shops of 60 bakers and 54 shoemakers and innumerable others, such as butchers, pastry cooks, masons, roofers, carpenters, jewelers, cutlers, hatters, painters, and tavernkeepers. This entire working population could be kept prosperous if the wholesale cloth merchants made the right decisions, buying wool at the lowest prices and finding the most advantageous markets for Beauvais cloth abroad. But the slightest depression in the world market could have terrible consequences for the city. Masters like Toupet may seem thinly insulated against sudden shifts in demand, but compared to their employees, the masters were well off. Woolworkers who did not own looms had no security at all. They worked for weekly wages that barely sufficed to pay for their rent, their taxes, and their daily bread. This in spite of a 12-hour workday with only two half-hour breaks for meals. With wages paid only for actual days worked, a few days' illness was enough to force a man into debt. Women earned very much less than men. It did not take much to push a woolworker into destitution.

Can it be that cities like Beauvais slipped from one subjection into another, having just barely achieved some autonomy from the limits of local resources, only to become slaves to the world economy? No doubt there is some truth to this proposition. We shall encounter cities whose growth was abruptly strangled because shifts occurred in trade patterns originating hundreds of miles away. More common is the case of the city that simply stagnates. But, taken together, the urban sector is privileged when compared to the peasant world. Unlike the surrounding countryside, cities are capable of growth. They can increase production to meet new demands. If hard times come, cities have far greater resources for dealing with scarcity than do mere villages. The commune has ways of protecting itself, of staying a step ahead of famine, ready to rescue its citizens, and even, when possible, of extending help to the peasants of the *tierra*.

Cities were giants in the marketplace. In times of scarcity, if it came to a contest between urban and rural consumers, the cities won hands down. Peasants could only glance anxiously at their fields, praying for rain, imploring their local saint to keep the frost away, calling in the village priest to exorcise a swarm of insects. When their harvest was ruined, they had to starve or flee. The entire drama of their fears and hopes was played out within the miniscule boundaries of their village territory. They had no way of foreseeing famine and they had no means of coping with it.[21]

Cities, on the contrary, could flex their communal muscles to great effect. One of the important functions of municipal government was to insure the steady availability of food at fixed prices. The great merchants in the city council had every reason to fear fluctuations in the price of bread and meat. Their own families were secure, and quite a number of lesser bourgeois households could depend on private stocks of grain and salted meat. But this was not true of the small masters, of the journeymen, tradesmen, and laborers who made up the largest portion of the population. Such people had no reserves of grain, no capital for stocking up against emergencies. They depended on daily purchases in the markets and shops. A poor harvest in the *tierra* could double and triple prices within weeks, while wages were hard to budge. In Beauvais, for instance, the wages of weavers remained almost constant in the seventeenth century. They were adequate wages for a healthy, single, male artisan, as long as the price of bread remained stable. If the weaver had a wife and children, he risked going hungry even in good times. Single women working for the masters of the wool trade earned only a third of the male weavers' wages. They could get by only if they pooled their resources, as did Françoise Boullet who shared a room near the cathedral in the old center of Beauvais with two other spinsters.

The great fear haunting all but the rich was the fear of scarcity, of poor harvests that would drive prices beyond the reach of ordinary people. Even the rumor of scarcity could be enough to provoke riots. The great merchants and bankers who controlled city government had every reason to wish for low food prices which would keep wages stable and prevent rebellion. The commune had powerful means available to this end. City treasuries could dispose of a great deal of capital derived both from municipal property assessments and sales taxes. These resources were put to good use. Grain was bought with public funds and stored in public silos. When prices rose, public grain was released to discourage speculation and hoarding. Municipal intervention could be triggered by seasonal shortages. Low grain prices were typical of early fall, soon after the harvest. By late spring, even in a good year, prices were likely to rise. This is when the public grain was offered for sale. An unusually bad harvest in the *tierra* could result in shortages and high prices as early as October. The city stepped in when this happened, offering grain to the bakers and seed to the farmers at subsidized rates. This happened in Valladolid, in 1567. By January of 1568, shortages were so acute that the city was selling enough subsidized grain to bake 10,000 pounds of bread every day. By February the quantity had doubled. In the course of the disastrous winter of 1594, Valladolid was selling enough cheap grain to the bakers to account for 24,000 pounds of bread daily while, at the same time, about 7,000 pounds daily were distributed at no charge, every day, both to the city's own poor and to the starving peasants of the *tierra*.

The resources needed for this kind of massive intervention were not easily assembled. Grain had to be bought and shipped in well in advance of potential harvest failures. Valladolid imported wheat for its municipal silos from as far away as Portugal, in spite of the fertility of its own *tierra*. The city of Valencia, whose grain silos, built in the sixteenth century, survived into the twentieth, was in the habit of sending grain buyers to Sicily. Such long-term, costly transactions called for contracts with specialized wholesalers and expensive financing. When local supplies were dangerously low and grain was expensive abroad, city treasurers would issue interest-bearing bonds to raise the necessary capital. Valencia had its own municipal bank which financed grain purchases in the world market. The price of bread was always the most important indicator and famine was the deadly enemy, but even in good times, and as a matter of course, the commune intervened in the marketplace so as to make sure that workers and paupers could afford to eat. This was done by means of leases, auctions, monopolies, and tax incentives whose combined effect was to make a public service of the urban food supply system.

The meat supply of Valladolid, for example, depended on a contract signed between the city council and a single contractor, the one who had turned in the lowest bid for a specified amount of meat to reach the city markets at fixed prices for the entire year. Such a contractor was referred to as the *obligado*, because he had obligated himself to supply the requisite provisions on stipulated terms. In exchange for guaranteed prices and supply, the commune conferred a monopoly upon the *obligado*. No other contractor was allowed to compete with him and even the retail butchers were forbidden to go out and buy cattle within a specified radius from the city limits. To make the contract even more attractive to the *obligado*, the meat he imported was free of taxes. Similar contracts were drawn up with other contractors for the supply of fish and other necessities. Occasionally, an *obligado* went bankrupt, caught between his contractual obligation and sudden price increases on the part of his suppliers. In times of scarcity, the city had to advance large sums to the *obligados*. Sometimes, unable to find a suitable bid, the city did its own procuring. In all such transactions, the policy of municipal governments remained constant. They assumed the responsibility of cushioning the members of the commune against scarcity and price rises.[22] In this respect, as in so many others, the bourgeois were better off than the peasants. If it is true that the urban commonwealth lived "magically outside of Nature's order," we must take a closer look at this magic, which cannot be reduced to economic advantages.

III

THE URBAN COMMUNITY

When compared to Asian or Middle Eastern urban centers, European cities were spectacularly independent. Their ability to escape the constraints of local resources was remarkable. They sent their wares wherever markets beckoned, creating demand if need be, selling arms in the Russian steppe, wine in the Caribbean, sugar in the Loire Valley. They minted coin, created banks and stock exchanges, insured maritime cargoes, dispatched ambassadors, maintained hotels and warehouses in distant lands.[1] Independent from the direct rule of kings as often as not, they guarded their freedom jealously, each city surrounding itself with fortificatons.

To the modern observer, a world filled with independent commonwealths of such small dimensions is something of a puzzle. A few thousand people, a few hundred acres, a moat, a gate, a bell tower, a marketplace: how could such small communities function without reference to larger authorities? Of course, each city was linked by roads and rivers to other cities and none, past a certain size, could have survived in economic isolation. Of course, there were royal, princely, imperial courts whose weight was felt by the communes. But it was not the distant prince who engaged the loyalty of the citizens. They did not think of themselves as Germans, Italians, or Spaniards so much as citizens of Nürnberg, Rotterdam, or Valencia.

The legitimacy of communal government did not depend on outside powers. Within the walls and beyond, throughout the *banlieue* or *termino* to the outer limits of their own *tierra*, communal governments reached every household, their authority unquestioned. Powers associated since the eighteenth century with the authority of national states were in the hands of local city officials before that time, including the power to make war, to execute criminals, to tax, to mint coin, to provide poor relief, to regulate religious worship, to provide formal education, to offer or to restrict the rights of citizenship, to repress insurrection. These powers were exercised without employing more than a handful of professional agents. The main responsibility for defense and police was assumed by the bourgeois themselves. They took turns standing guard. They rushed to the armory in time of emergency. Municipal supervisors of hospitals and poorhouses were prominent citizens appointed for this purpose. City business was often conducted on Sundays, when merchants and artisans could spare the time. A few specialists worked on a retainer fee basis: the public executioner, the municipal doctor, the city architect, the city attorney. Otherwise, the apparatus of government could be described as consisting largely of citizen volunteers.[2]

Early modern cities were able to command the allegiance of their citizens to an extent that is hard to imagine in a modern setting, even though the differences separating the rich from the poor were profound and very much visible and openly discussed. The mayor of the city of Bordeaux, writing around 1580, reports a conversation he claims to have had with an American Indian chief who had been brought to the French seaport city of Rouen. What struck him as most remarkable about European cities? the Indian chief was asked through an interpreter. Without hesitation, this visitor from another world is said to have replied that he was astounded by the contrast he observed in the streets of Rouen between fat, warmly dressed people on the one hand, and on the other, the mass of half-starved men and women wearing clothes that were not much better than rags. He could not understand, said the Indian, why the starving ones did not grab the fat ones by the throat.[3]

The mayor of Bordeaux was by no means alone in commenting in this oblique manner on the uneven distribution of wealth in European cities and on the remarkable fact that distress did not lead to insurrection. On the whole, the authority of communal government was accepted. This can be understood only if we look at the commune as something more than a purely administrative system.

It would be best, probably, to forget what a modern city is, if we want to understand a sixteenth-century commune. As Charles Pythian-Adams explains, in his fine study of the English city of Coventry, living in a sixteenth-century city was more like being enrolled in a school, college, or regiment, because everyone's waking hours were continuously occupied in prescribed ways and the place of every individual was more precisely and formally defined than it is in a modern city.[4]

It was defined, first of all, at the level of the family. A family came into being by means of a contract between two consenting adults. Such a contract could be a simple verbal agreement. In the case of partners endowed with sufficient property, the union was sealed by means of a written agreement, duly witnessed and notarized. In either case, the couple was considered married even before the wedding had taken place. Marriages were not usually arranged by the couple's parents. Husband and wife formed a partnership that remained independent of the larger circle of relatives. The new couple did not usually move in with in-laws. They established their own household. The new wife was not a child or an adolescent, as was the case in non-European societies. She was an adult woman in her twenties whose contract was with her new husband alone. If the bride brought a dowry, it was paid to the husband rather than to the husband's parents. If the husband died, the children accompanied their mother on her remarriage. In sum, the modern Western family was fully in existence by the sixteenth century. It consisted of a couple and their eventual children. In Coventry, a census taken in 1523 records only three cases, out of a total of 1,302 households surveyed, in which any relatives are living with the couple.[5]

Marriage was the most important event in an individual's career. Before marriage, both men and women remained dependents, their status not markedly different from that of servants. They worked either for their own parents or for the master and mistress of another household. As serving maids or apprentices, adolescents were bound to their masters who were permitted to take them on only on condition that they kept them in their own houses, providing "meate, drynke and lodgynge" and exercising full authority over them. Release from this dependence could be achieved only through marriage. Few single men could afford to set up shop on their own. They needed a woman's help in their work. Bachelors were not in a position to take on apprentices, since they lacked a wife who could run the household. Some Crafts specifically ruled that "no yong man unmarried take any prentys till he have occupied 3 years at the least."

The formation of a new family was directly linked to the establishment of a new unit of production, among urban artisans as well as among farmers. Weddings were attended by all the masters of the groom's Craft. In a sense, the new bride was accepted into the Craft fellowship. The butchers and the tilers of Coventry, for instance, described their members as brothers and sisters. Although the new bride was not likely to possess the skills of the Craft, she might learn them in time. Technical secrets were jealously guarded, but an exception could be made for the masters' wives. The cappers' fellowship of Coventry, for instance, expressly forbade each master to teach his skills to any person "save to his prentiz and his wyf." When a master died, his widow continued to supervise the work of the journeymen and apprentices. But this was a temporary state of affairs. When a son had completed his apprenticeship, he would replace his mother at the head of the enterprise. Widows could remarry, to be sure, but unless they were young, attractive, or wealthy, their chances of finding a new husband were slim. There were nine times as many widows as widowers heading households in Coventry. Roughly half of these widows lived alone, often in extreme poverty. There was no comfortable place for single persons in an early modern city. Women under the age of 50 were actually forbidden, in Coventry, to set up house on their own. They were required to share quarters with other spinsters. Aside from elderly widows, hardly anyone lived alone. Few people could escape membership in a household where everyone's status was defined. Wives, apprentices, journeymen, and servants all had a particular place within the household, a place at times contractually spelled out. Journeymen were protected against tyrannical masters through the mediation of the Craft. A weaver's journeyman could strike if his wages were left unpaid. In such a case, "his loome schall not goo but stond styll."

Although each household was independent as a family unit, it belonged to the larger solidarity of the Craft. No individual could be said to participate fully in the life of the city except as a member of a household: it was the household that was taxed, it was the household that was called upon for military service. Households, in turn, could not stand alone. In many cities it was the Craft fellowship, through its elected officers, that divided the tax burden among its member households. When it came to providing soldiers, it was not uncommon for the Crafts to organize the muster. The Craft masters were present at weddings, when a new family was formed, and present, again, at funerals, when a family was dissolved. The Crafts regulated relations between masters and journeymen, they set the conditions of apprenticeship, they resolved disputes between rival masters, they collected dues, set minimum prices and wages, and watched over the protection of trade secrets. Members of a Craft fellowship, once initiated into the mysteries of their Craft, were forbidden to "disclose nor utter no thynges that ought of right to be secretly kept amonges them-selves." Only in this way, it was thought, could "unytie in all fellowships and companyes . . . be kept and preserved."

The preservation of unity among all the householders associated within a given Craft was one of the chief aims pursued by the members. They met together, several times a year, to feast and drink. On holidays, when the commune organized processions and pageants, each Craft fellowship marched as a body, attired in special costumes. A family's status in the city was largely derived from its membership in a given Craft—and within the fellowships and companies each member could look forward to a well-regulated rise in his own career. Coventry's master carpenters, for instance, could expect to be elected to junior office in the Craft some six years after setting up shop, on the average, and to senior office about eight years later.

This is not to say that the Craft system promoted equality. Each Craft had a specific place in the city's hierarchy, a place jealously guarded and publicly acknowledged. Drapers were more important than butchers in a city like Coventry. Within the Craft, rich masters rose more quickly to high office than did poor ones. As for journeymen, they were separated from the masters who employed them. But the Craft system did provide a sense of belonging to the community. It provided an opportunity, even for journeymen, to rise, step by step, along the ladder which led to recognition, honors, and power. Journeymen were not always and everywhere as well-integrated into the Craft system as they were in sixteenth-century Coventry, but the example of Coventry is a good starting point. It allows us to understand the ideal of a socially integrated community inherited from earlier times. In larger cities, in cities with a more complex industrial organization, masters and journeymen could easily become adversary groups. In the case of Coventry, by no means an exceptional case, journeymen had a stake in the established order. They had their own fellowship associations which paralleled the masters' fellowships. They even had a good chance of becoming masters. Pythian-Adams estimates that as many as half of Coventry's journeymen were able, sooner or later, to rise to the position of master of the Craft. This is not surprising, since the ratio of journeymen to masters in the Coventry Crafts seemed designed to allow for the replacement of retiring or ailing masters. In 1547, for example, there were 47 journeymen for 63 masters in the cappers' craft. In 1522, 45 journeymen for 37 masters in the weavers' craft.

From the journeyman who hoped to become a master, to the established master in one of the less prestigious Crafts who looked forward to holding office in his fellowship, the ladder of social rank led up to the most prosperous masters in the more influential Crafts. Such men would expect to graduate from senior Craft office to the pinnacle of power and dignity in the city. They were candidates for elective office in city hall. The transition from Craft office to public office was prepared through membership in city-wide religious brotherhoods that embraced all the Crafts. In Coventry there were two such brotherhoods, the Corpus Christi guild and Holy Trinity guild. Corpus Christi was responsible for arranging the procession on Corpus Christi day, the most important ceremonial event of the year. Corpus Christi membership was fairly broad. In 1520, the guild had 282 members, that is to say, close to half the masters in the city. Holy Trinity was more exclusive. The élite of the city moved from Craft office to membership in Corpus Christi, then on to Holy Trinity and election to the common council of the commune, which had a membership of 48—and, finally, to the senior council, with a membership of 12, which included the mayor and the aldermen.[6]

Not all residents were embraced by this system of graduated honors, even in a tight little community like Coventry. At least one fifth of the inhabitants were left out of the Craft system and denied a place in the city's power structure. But even servants and common laborers experienced membership in the community in a number of ways. Enclosed by the city's protective walls, their workday regulated by the city's ordinances, they bought their provisions in the city's markets at preferential prices not available to outsiders and they participated in the commune's numerous public festivities. They were incorporated into the city's obligatory rhythms.

At 4:00 A.M., the day bell was rung in the parish churches. The night watch stood down. The city gates were opened. Carpenters, tilers, masons, and laborers appeared with their tools in the city's central crossroads at 5:00 A.M., hoping for work. By 7:00 P.M., the workday was over. At 8:00, curfew was imposed, the gates were locked, the night watch was assembled, innkeepers extinguished the lanterns which were hung outside their doors. On Saturdays, when workmen were paid their week's wages, work stopped earlier. There was time to visit the alehouses. Householders swept the streets in front of their lodgings. Sunday was a day of rest, graced by the alternating and competing entertainments to be found in religious observances, drinking, and sports. The better sort of people, including the mayor, the aldermen, and the officers of the guilds and Crafts, were sure to be found in church, sporting their colorful robes of office. Less respectable members of the community, on the other hand, were tempted by "brekefastes or drynkynges at Matyns, high masse or evensong tymes," in spite of official prohibitions. There were shopkeepers who kept their doors open on Sundays, even "in tyme of dyvyne service."[7]

The "unytie" of the Craft fellowships bound workingmen together. Women and children remained on the periphery of these occupational and religious fraternities, but there was another kind of association which included everyone. This was the formal association of the neighborhood.

Wards were organized for purposes of taxation, firefighting, guard duty, and other manifestations of civic-mindedness. Each ward had a character of its own. There were wards, usually in the center of town, near the cathedral and city hall, in which the wealthiest families were likely to congregate. Some wards were marked by concentrations of certain trades, those of the butchers, tanners, and dyers, for instance, whose houses were, inevitably, located along a river. In spite of such differences, rich householders lived side by side with poor ones. The example of Coventry, where cheap housing was fairly evenly spread in most wards, can be taken as fairly typical.

The wealthy cloth merchant who held office in the drapers' fellowship was also a member of a ward organization that cut across the divisions of wealth, occupation, rank, and family relations. There was nothing casual about regular service in militia units organized by street and neighborhood. An extreme example of a city where ward membership has provoked passionate feelings since the thirteenth century is that of the Italian city of Siena. Each Sienese ward still has its own flag today, its colors, its symbols. There is the ward of the Eagle, the ward of the Snail, Owl, Tortoise, Giraffe, Goose—and so on. The modern Siennese still know precisely where the boundaries of their wards are drawn. Being "of the Goose" or "of the Giraffe" is a matter of great importance in Siena. Children are brought up to be proud of their own ward and contemptuous of rival ones. A Giraffe mother will spoon-feed her baby, saying "One for mummy, one for daddy, one for the Giraffe." The same mother will then condition the child to dislike the rival ward of the Caterpillar by saying: "And this is for the Caterpillar," only to withdraw the spoon quickly, just as the baby opens its mouth. A two-year-old boy wearing a scarf with the Caterpillar colors is asked his name. "Marco," he says. "And how old are you?" is the next question. Marco holds up two fingers. Then he is asked: "How is the Caterpillar?" "*Bello* [It is beautiful]," he replies. "And what about the Giraffe?" "It stinks," says the child.

The rivalry between the wards of Siena culminates, every year, in a horse race run on the main piazza. This race, in which the jockeys wear the colors of the competing wards, is dedicated to the Virgin Mary. It mobilizes the entire population of the city for weeks before the great event. Siena is exceptional only because the medieval tradition of the annual race has survived into the late twentieth century. In many cities similar races and equally passionate rivalries between wards were still customary a century ago.

The important difference between the ward and other social associations is that the ward encompasses all those who are born in it, regardless of individual differences of wealth and occupation. The ward complemented the other associations, allowing rich and poor to mingle on an equal footing, enrolling men, women, and children in a common purpose, linking butchers, bankers, and laborers in a fraternity which demanded no dues. Although rivalry between the wards could get out of hand, as it still does in Siena, when young men get involved in brawls during the feverish hours preceding the race, the commune controlled the wards, much as it controlled the Crafts, by means of interlocking directorates of elected officials. In Siena, each ward has its own general assembly which elects officers who represent the ward in a city-wide committee. On the day of the race, when banquets, processions, much drinking, cheering, and fighting are bound to raise tempers, the commune and the clergy control events. The horses are blessed by priests and assigned to each ward in a public ceremony over which the mayor presides.[8]

At work or at play, the citizens were never far from the watchful gaze of the city fathers. Every clue to potential trouble triggered rules and ordinances whose overall intent was to flush secret discontent into the open, where it could be seen and managed. A perfect illustration of these procedures is to be found in the municipal management of sexuality.

In a society where marriage came rather late for most people—and especially late for the poor—there was always a large pool of unmarried young men who presented a clear and present danger to morality: apprentices, journeymen, male servants, and sons of masters waiting for the day when they could have a wife and a shop of their own. Marriage without financial security was unthinkable. Servants were sometimes not even permitted to marry. In some cities a minimum age requirement was stipulated and city council approval was needed if one wished to marry sooner. Then, there were those who had no expectation of ever contracting marriage: vagrants, soldiers, peddlers, clergy. Altogether, a huge number of single men in their twenties who eyed the wives and daughters of established bourgeois ferociously. Even though unmarried men were closely watched by fathers and masters—and in the case of monks, by their abbots and priors—there were opportunities, especially on holidays, for bachelors to show their frustration and their resentment. In the French city of Dijon, for instance, in 1505, we can eavesdrop on two journeymen masons who are watching a pretty sixteen-year-old girl of good family walk past. Perhaps the men had been drinking. In any case, they could not control themselves. "We'll fuck you," they yell. "We can fuck you as well as anybody!"[9]

The two young masons were only saying what must have been on the mind of many unmarried young males in the city. They were feeling deprived. They resented the enormous privilege of the older, richer men who never slept alone. And they watched over the city's young women with a jealous zeal, knowing that they might have to wait ten years or longer before they had a chance to propose marriage. Meanwhile, rich masters had their pick, claiming young girls as their wives. Well-established widowers who remarried provoked the anger of single men by removing more young women from the pool of those potentially available for marriage.

This rivalry between young and old males expressed itself in various forms of violence. Rape was a common occurrence, and it followed a particular pattern, revealing the frustrations of unmarried males. Most of the recorded cases of rape in Dijon, for instance, were calculated outrages perpetrated, not by individuals, but by groups of young men. The victims were women between the ages of 15 and 30. They were likely to be servant girls of whom it was rumored that they slept with their masters, priests' concubines, young widows, wives whose husbands were away. Gangs of rowdy young men descended on these women, broke down their doors, terrified the neighbors, and raped the victim repeatedly, while shouting curses. The aggressors were not vagrants or hooligans who seized a passing chance at mayhem, but members of the community, in good standing, who participated in a premeditated assault. They were, in most cases, journeymen, servants, or sons of masters between the ages of 18 and 24. There were about 20 such gang rapes in a city like Dijon every year. Almost 100 young men were implicated in these crimes annually. Perhaps half the males in the city had been involved in group rapes of this sort before reaching maturity.

Needless to say, the municipal authorities did not take kindly to such disturbances. Recogizing the problem, the city fathers made provisions for satisfying the sexual needs of unmarried men. The obvious solution was the establishment of a municipal brothel. Such brothels could be anything from a simple four-bedroom house with a garden, in a small town like Tarascon, to a splendid mansion with 20 bedrooms in Dijon, or even a block of buildings, an entire ghetto for prostitution, in busy commercial centers like Lyon or in cities filled with priests, like Avignon. The public brothel was not a cause for shame in the community. Operating under municipal license, the manager was obliged to follow rules laid down in city hall. Brothels were not, in principle, open to married men or priests. When contagious diseases threatened, the brothel was closed down. In normal times, the establishment provided cheap sex and good cheer. In exchange for low prices and approved women, the brothel operator was allowed to make considerable profits on his sale of food and drink to his clients.

The public brothel was a place of last resort where a journeyman could find solace for a few pennies and thus be deflected from engaging in violence and committing public outrages. A man with more money to spend could pick up prettier and younger prostitutes who free-lanced in streets and inns—or else he could frequent the municipal bathhouse, a thinly disguised but rather expensive massage parlor which offered younger girls ("bath attendants") and more discretion than was to be expected from the brothel. Dijon's famous bathhouse catered to a select clientele comprising large numbers of priests. These profitable semipublic institutions were licensed, supervised, and regulated by the city. Free-lance prostitutes, just starting out on their careers, wore a special badge, certifying that they had paid the city license fee and that they came under the city's official protection. A few years later, at about age 20, the same prostitute was likely to be found working as a bath attendant in bathhouses with more bedding than baths. Later on still, she would find her way to the brothel. All the while, she was protected by the authorities. When she retired, at last, at about age 30, it was not unheard of to find a prostitute pensioned off, the city having found a husband and provided a dowry.

This system of licensed prostitution is a clear instance of the communes' attempts at managing even the most intimate aspects of the citizens' lives. Not content with making provisions for the satisfaction of physical needs, the commune intervened also at the psychological level, since young males resented the sexual privileges of their elders, in spite of the availability of commercial sex. This resentment was openly expressed by youth clubs formed in the wards or in the shadow of Craft fellowships. Every city had such clubs, often referred to as Abbeys of Youth. These clubs enrolled mostly young, unmarried male members of the community. Organized along the lines of other communal associations, the clubs elected officers with grandiose and mocking titles, abbots of misrule, abbots of gaiety, princes of pleasure, and princes of fools. The chief purpose of these youth associations was to safeguard the collective rights of single men over the city's marriageable young women. The Abbeys of Fools appeared at weddings, wearing odd costumes, singing, cheering, making provocative speeches, and demanding to be paid off in exchange for letting the marriage proceed. The main targets of the youth clubs' aggressive noisemaking were older men who took young wives—and outsiders, men from beyond the limits of the ward or even from out of town, who presumed to take away marriageable girls. Against such raiders of their womenfolk, the youth clubs mounted savage attacks in the form of satirical plays, in song and verse, depicting the intruders and rivals as impotent old men who would not be able to satisfy their brides' vigorous sexual appetites.

The youth clubs became especially riotous at carnival time, but the city fathers tolerated their antics, acting on the prudent premise that "it is sometimes expedient to allow the people to play the fool and make merry, lest by holding them in with too great a rigor, we put them in despair."[10] This astute observation, made by a prominent citizen of Lyon, should suffice to remind us that the youth clubs could become dangerous to public order. As long as they demonstrated only to protest against older men who took young wives, they were tolerated. But when sexual envy turned to social protest, the city could cancel the clubs' marching permits in the carnival parade. In ordinary times, the youth clubs were integrated into the community. Their performances on public occasions were rowdy, but this was countenanced. Some of the fines the clubs extorted from elderly bridegrooms were turned over to city hall. The elections of Princes of Youth were sometimes monitored by city officials. In times of war, the youth clubs served the commune as militia units. In this way, even the most volatile elements of the population could be restrained and even the deepest frustrations could be deflected from becoming challenges to authority.

IV

THE URBAN ELITE

"What Emperor? We are the Emperor here—and the Emperor is Emperor in Vienna."[1]

In stressing the self-contained nature of the urban community, its independence from external sources of legitimacy, the importance of occupational, religious, and neighborhood associations and the effectiveness of city government, we run the risk of describing the urban community as contemporaries wished it to be, rather than as it really was.

The ramparts of the medieval city remained in place, the Craft fellowships, the religious brotherhoods, and the ward associations continued to function and municipal governments continued to exercise their authority firmly, but the unity of the commune came under assault from several directions, especially in the sixteenth century, and more so in major cities than in smaller towns.

Heresy, immigration, and royal interference were powerful stimuli that penetrated the protective fabric of urban communities like so many sticks poked into anthills. It was difficult to maintain the unity of the commune when its members were prepared to kill each other over their conflicting interpretations of Holy Scripture. As Europe became divided between Catholics, Lutherans, Calvinists, and other religious sects, tension grew. The population growth and the economic vitality of the age pushed millions of immigrants into the cities. These immigrants, coming from the countryside or fleeing religious persecution, were needed in the urban labor force. Their skills and their capital were welcome. But they were not easily integrated into the community. Royal governments, which, in the past, had been satisfied with a largely ceremonial role, began to raise taxes and to conduct large-scale wars. The cost of these wars saddled most cities with heavy debts and threatened their ancient tradition of autonomy.

The commune could burn heretics, close its gates to foreigners, even resist the peremptory commands of princes. The gravest danger to its ancient constitution, however, was an internal threat against which no remedies proved effective. Unlike the plague, against which quarantines could be imposed, unlike the armies of the poor which could be shut out, the new challenge came from the very heart of the community. It took the form of a gradual transformation of urban society which was to diminish the sense of common purpose and shared power that had been the essence of the medieval city.

The simplest way to describe this development is to say that the rich usurped all power within the cities. Such a formulation may serve as the starting point of our analysis and it may explain why the long process of usurpation encountered little resistance at first. After all, the rich had dominated urban politics all along. If we take a close look at an ordinary city, we may not notice much beyond an increasing concentration of political power in the hands of the richest families. The medieval constitution of the commune was usually left intact. In principle, every male citizen remained eligible for office.

Take the example of the German city of Nördlingen, studied by Christopher Friedrichs.[2] Nördlingen, a city comparable to Coventry, housed about 7,000 people within its walls. It was governed by an elected council of fifteen. As late as 1580, those all-powerful magistrates remained reasonably representative of the community: five were masters of their Crafts, another five were merchants. Some belonged to the wealthiest families in town, others were men of more modest means. Some were well connected, their relatives having served as councillors before them, but there was room for new men too.

That was the situation in 1580. In the course of the next century, master craftsmen and shopkeepers disappeared from the city council. Although every male citizen continued to be eligible for office, in practice the council learned to manipulate the constitution so as to restrict membership to the wealthy. We cannot speak of a closed élite, as yet. It was still possible, exceptionally, for a man of modest origin who succeeded in his trade, to reach high office. This is what happened in the case of Samuel Dehlinger, a tanner worth only 100 florins in 1646. By 1658, he was worth 1,400 florins, still a modest estate, but a sufficient warranty of reliability, it seems, since Dehlinger reached council office in 1675. His fortune was just barely adequate. There might be one or two others of similar standing in the council, but the significant fact is that at least 10 of the 15 councillors, consistently, came from the richest 5 percent of the citizenry. When you consider that the 15 members of the council, collectively, owned 9 percent of the total assessed wealth attributed to 1,541 taxpaying households in 1579—and that this share was to increase to 30 percent by 1646—there is no escaping the conclusion that the richest families in Nördlingen were achieving control of the city.

The exclusion of artisans and shopkeepers from the city council cannot be understood without going back to a constitutional revolution that occurred in Nördlingen, as it did in many other cities, in the sixteenth century. Until 1552, Nördlingen had been governed by a council of 24, half of whose membership necessarily represented the Crafts of the city. In that year, the ancient link between the Crafts and city government was severed. Tanners, butchers, and other artisans remained eligible for council office as individuals, but the commune ceased being the collective expression of the Crafts. There had been a time when no one could imagine being a member of the commune without being, at the same time, a member of a Craft. That time was past. There were citizens, now, who achieved great wealth without practicing a craft or owning a shop. Wholesale merchants replaced shopkeepers and artisans in the city council. Soon even wholesale merchants would be displaced by a new breed of men who were rich without actually engaging in trade.

This development is best studied in cities endowed with greated economic importance than either Nördlingen or Coventry could claim. A good example is provided by Frankfurt, a city about three times the size of Nördlingen, situated on the Main River, at the intersection of important trade routes. Frankfurt produced almost nothing for export. Its prosperity was due to international commerce and banking. A city of some 20,000 inhabitants, it was top heavy with wholesale merchants and financiers. It was also packed full of foreigners. Perhaps as many as half of the inhabitants were not native-born citizens. Frankfurt may serve as a case study of the social changes experienced by cities that embraced the new economic opportunities of the sixteenth century.

Unlike Coventry or Beauvais, Frankfurt no longer fitted the traditional pattern of a medieval city whose energies were devoted to the production of cloth and of other goods for export. The artisans of Frankfurt were content with supplying local needs. Since the prosperity of the city did not depend on its artisans, it is not surprising that the Crafts of Frankfurt lost their connection with city government quite early. Bewildered by their exclusion from the political process, Frankfurt's artisans expressed their resentment in several ways, including armed revolt. Such revolts, the last one occurring in the summer of 1614, ended in failure. The leaders of the rioting artisans were executed and the wealthy families of Frankfurt held on to their power more rigidly than ever. Failing to comprehend the changes that had eroded the political power of the working population, rebellious artisans insisted on such notions as the requirement that all citizens should be members of a craft. Although their resentment was directed against the leading families which controlled city hall, they also felt threatened by various categories of immigrants who were allowed to live in the city under the council's protection, including a large Jewish community which was plundered in the course of the riots of 1614.

Artisans were not the only group excluded from power in Frankfurt. The medieval vision of the urban commune as a sworn association of native craftsmen and merchants was sorely tried here, where the foreign-born at times threatened to outnumber native citizens. Foreigners in Frankfurt could no longer be considered an anomaly. They were more than a marginal group of laborers who would return to their villages some day or become assimilated into the urban community. Foreigners were essential to Frankfurt's commerce. A good many were Calvinists who had fled persecution in the Low Countries. They came with their capital, their skills, their international connections—as did the Jews. In both cases, integration was out of the question. Frankfurt was a Lutheran city. Admission to citizenship was open only to Lutherans. As a result, the social and political complexion of the city appeared distorted to those who persisted in using the medieval ideal of a community as a standard. Here, Calvinists, Jews, and Catholics lived side by side with Lutherans and native citizens lived next to foreigners who did not share in the obligations and privileges of citizenship. Instead of becoming united with native *Bürger* in Craft fellowships and religious brotherhoods, immigrant families were linked to the commune exclusively through their subjection to the city council. The Jewish community, several thousand strong, exhibited its separate status most visibly, enclosed as it was in a ghetto. Other categories of tolerated residents were also deprived of civic rights. Foreigners *(Fremde)* who showed no interest in becoming permanent settlers were allowed to rent lodgings only after registering with a special office in city hall. Other foreigners petitioned the council for permission to establish permanent residence. If their petition was granted, they swore an oath of allegiance and paid taxes, but they did not acquire the right of citizenship, even after years of residence. As tolerated residents *(Beisassen)*, they did not become members of the community. Forbidden to buy real estate, they were also excluded from membership in the Crafts. As a result, there were several separate communities coexisting in the city, powerless, all of them, vis-à-vis the city council, albeit in varying degrees. Christian *Fremde* had more rights than Jewish ones, Lutherans were more privileged than were Calvinists, *Beisassen* were less ill at ease than were *Fremde*—but even the *Bürger*, the core of native-born citizens whose privileges exceeded those of other groups—even they were, in fact, excluded from power.

That artisans could be informally kept from reaching high office is not very surprising. In Frankfurt, however, even wealthy merchants were similarly excluded. Instead of pointing to his honorable reputation as a master craftsman, or to his enviable success in business, the candidate for high office in Frankfurt had to convince his peers that, on the contrary, neither he nor his father or grandfather before him ever practiced a craft or sold goods in a shop. The medieval values of the commune, in sum, had been turned upside down. Instead of taking pride in work, the élite of Frankfurt prided itself on having left work behind.

We will soon discover that such attitudes were common among the bourgeois élites of most other major cities. Frankfurt's élite was unusual only because of the formal manner in which it chose to mark the difference between itself and the common citizens. In all other respects, the "well-born families" *(Geschlechter)* that governed Frankfurt acted as did urban élites everywhere. After achieving wealth as merchants, they withdrew from commerce, invested their capital in farmland, urban real estate, banking, and office, began claiming noble status, married within the select circle of families of similar standing, and found ways, sometimes with the help of princes, of subverting the communal constitution to their own advantage.

Frankfurt's élite consisted of some 45 families, less than 1 percent of the population. This small group retained exclusive control of the 15 top offices from the fourteenth to the eighteenth centuries and it invented elaborate associations to safeguard its position in the city. Inasmuch as carpenters or shoemakers were united in fellowships, there was no reason why the *Geschlechter* should be deprived of the pleasures and advantages of belonging to formal fellowships. They were specialists, too, after all. It is true that their specialty was a new one. They did not make shoes or cloth, they had no shops, no painted signs hung from their lodgings, proclaiming their skills. Their craft was statecraft, their art the art of governing. They claimed that governing a city was specialized work for which one had to be suitably trained, and they established associations on the pattern of the Craft fellowships, to retain the monopoly of their own craft by excluding non-members from government office.

The most prestigious of these curious fellowships in Frankfurt was the Alt-Limpurg Society. Of fourteenth-century origin, this exclusive club admitted few new families to membership after the mid-sixteenth century. Although the families associated in the Alt-Limpurg Society had all made their fortunes, originally, in commerce, they began to deny their bourgeois origins, they acquired coats of arms and refused to admit merchants to membership. A second club, the Frauenstein Society, may have been a little less squeamish about admitting wealthy wholesale merchants, but, taken together, the Limpurger and Frauensteiner appeared to contemporaries as an exclusive and aristocratic élite of ancient extraction.[3]

Frankfurt's *Geschlechter* ruled the city by resorting to the methods employed by urban élites everywhere. They could count on the admiration of the *Bürger*. They knew how to maintain the appearance of shared power by appointing *Bürger* to second-rank positions in city government. Above all, they had mastered the secret of maintaining their wealth while avoiding direct involvement in commerce.

Not only modern historians, but even their fellow citizens were puzzled, on occasion, by the mysterious ways in which a handful of families remained wealthy, generation after generation, without being engaged, visibly, in any conventional form of profit-making. Butchers, weavers, tanners, dyers, or hatmakers can hardly be blamed for being suspicious of families that remained wealthy even though they produced nothing and sold nothing. To people accustomed to judge their neighbor's prosperity by counting bolts of cloth sold and barrels of wine shipped abroad, the fortunes of the élite were bound to appear mysterious. They cannot be understood at all, without reference to national and territorial governments that had hardly existed before the fifteenth century.

When kings acquired the power to levy permanent taxes on their subjects, the richest merchants found it more profitable to lend money to royal treasuries than to invest in commerce. A special, and mutually profitable, relationship soon developed between urban élites and royal governments. The princes of the Roman Church had been pioneers in this respect. Secular rulers merely followed their early lead. Popes and kings claimed the right to tax their subjects, but they were not equipped to enforce their rights. Perpetually short of funds, spending on a lavish scale, they borrowed at high rates of interest, using their right to collect taxes as collateral.

Drapers, mercers, wine merchants, goldsmiths, and others with capital to invest had discovered, long ago, that diversification was prudent, especially when wars disrupted trade routes. They had learned to invest in land and urban real estate. The return on such investments was not dramatic, but it was steady and reliable. The characteristic method used in such investments was an unwieldy and secretive arrangement called a *rente* in French-speaking regions. Investors advanced a sum of money to a landowner in need of cash. Not openly described as a loan, the *rente* entitled the investor to receive fixed annual payments, something on the order of 10 percent of the sum originally advanced. In theory, the merchant who advanced 40 pounds to a starving peasant or to a bankrupt gentleman, became a shareholder in an agricultural enterprise. By virtue of legally binding contracts, he was entitled to receive 4 pounds yearly from the farmer. If payment was late, fines were added on. A peasant in difficulty was forced to renegotiate his *rente* on the worst of terms. Eventually, the struggling debtor had no choice but to sign further *rentes*, alienating additional portions of his land. Sooner or later there would be nothing left to call his own.

Having learned how profitable such investments could be in the long run, wealthy merchants were tempted to become *rentiers*. They soon found even more profitable terms when they applied the principle of the *rente* to goverment lending. Kings needed large sums in a hurry. To finance their wars, they sold *rentes*. Royal *rentes*, secured by the future income of taxes, were bought up by investors even though the interest rate was modest. French royal *rentes*, for instance, habitually yielded no more than 8.3 percent annually. The same people who drew interest from *rentes* paid by peasants and other private borrowers also drew interest from public *rentes*, royal or municipal. The *rente*-holders' status as creditors to kings generated other opportunities for them. Soon *rentiers* were contracting for the right to collect taxes in the king's name, a most profitable activity called tax-farming.

All this sounds simpler than it was. Anyone could buy a *rente*, but as soon as *rentiers* began acting in an official capacity, representing the government as tax collectors and arbitrating tax disputes, more than money was involved. Tens of thousands of officials were soon needed to enforce the royal will. Becoming an official was to be the goal of every ambitious bourgeois in Europe. This took capital, to be sure, since almost all official positions were for sale. But capital alone did not suffice. Formal education was another necessity. The *rentier* equipped with a law degree was ready to leave commerce behind and to start climbing the ladder of success in the service of his king.

When the *Geschlechter* in Frankfurt closed ranks, they may have appeared merely snobbish. In reality, their actions were perfectly rational.

To achieve success in the world of officeholding, they needed to shift their capital away from commerce, they needed to appear noble, they had to acquire a new kind of formal education, and they had to cultivate alliances with other influential families. In all these respects they were behaving exactly like their French or Spanish counterparts. If anything, such developments in German cities were pale imitations of what was happening in countries with more fully developed national bureaucracies.

The example of Valladolid is particularly instructive in this respect. Here the opportunities for the officeholding élite were especially ample, because the city served as the capital of the Kingdom of Castile before Phillip II transferred his court to Madrid. The *rentiers* of Valladolid were in a good position to exploit the entire Spanish empire. As a result, Valladolid was becoming a city in which production of goods was a minority activity. In the mid-sixteenth century, only 2,425 households out of 6,652 can be clearly linked to some sort of productive activity in Valladolid. No more than 40 percent of the inhabitants could be described as working, in one way or another. In 1570, there were 673 households of workers—*trabajadores*—while 1,870 households, a staggering figure, were headed by *oficiales*. Merchants occupied a secondary position. The richest, the most powerful, and the most privileged families in Valladolid were variously described as being headed by *oficiales, caballeros,* or *letrados.* This group included lawyers, physicians, and judges, as well as large numbers of men who did not exercise a profession, although they had university degrees. Such *letrados* (men of letters, university graduates) and *caballeros* (gentlemen) claimed some of the privileges associated with nobility, including tax exemption. These claims rested on the proven fact of their wealth and leisure.

Their wealth was typical *rentier* wealth. They drew income from private *rentes,* known as *censos* in Castile, which paid 7.14 percent. Government *rentes (juros)* were also important in the portfolios of *letrados, caballeros,* and *oficiales.* A particularly striking illustration of the importance of *juros* in the Spanish economy is provided by Professor Bennassar's calculations. He estimates that the amount of money paid each year by all the inhabitants of Valladolid in sales taxes to the national government was roughly equal to the amount returned to Valladolid *rentiers* in interest payments on *juros.* Which explains why the Spanish government was always near bankruptcy, in spite of impressive tax collections: ordinary people paid taxes so that the government debts to the local élite could be serviced.[4]

In the right hands, a portfolio of *rentes* could become far more valuable than a warehouse filled with casks of wine. The first step in the making of a *rentier* was likely to be the purchase of land, if possible, noble land. Rich merchants looked for such opportunities. By means of *rente* contracts, they sought to buy their way into an estate owned by an impoverished aristocrat. Failing that, an ordinary farm would do. In time, old farm buildings could be remodeled. The addition of a tower in one corner, of a stone bridge, a moat, a dovecote, might suffice to transform a plain farmhouse into something resembling a castle. Soon the wine merchant would learn to play the part of the country gentleman. His son would be steered away from the family business. Destined for paperwork, he would be sent to schools designed to produce future lawyers and officeholders. Years later, after completing his studies at the university, the young man returned, ready for marriage. The marriage contract might well include not only land, real estate, and cash, settled on the young couple, but also surely various *rentes* as well and the promise of a judgeship or similar office to be passed on, eventually, by the father-in-law. At the third generation, the process being repeated, we will encounter men who no longer had any direct memories of the merchant's life. They created their own lifestyle, their own culture, different from that of the bourgeois, and different, as well, from the values of the nobility.[5]

Understanding this development ought to be one of the very first priorities of the social historian. Contemporaries struggled to understand what was happening. The more astute observers among them did notice that a new class was born, an élite of highly educated *rentiers*, of capitalists in government service who should not be confused with the old feudal élite of landed warriors. Even the most flexible minds, however, found it difficult to fit this new class into the existing framework of social analysis.

Medieval political theory spoke loosely of Three Orders or Estates. The clergy was described as the First Estate, the nobility as the Second, while all others, merchants, artisans, and peasants among them, were unceremoniously relegated to the Third or last Estate. This ancient scheme had the advantage of being simple, but it hardly corresponded to reality. To treat the clergy as a homogeneous group was pure fantasy, since priests, monks, and nuns did not form families and could not transmit their status to the following generation. The clerical First Estate was a false category. It was made up of a mass of country priests recruited from the so-called Third Estate and it was led by an élite of abbots and bishops of noble or rich commoner origin.

There were contemporaries who saw this quite clearly. They concluded that there were really only "two kinds of persons: the first kind are nobles; the second commoners." This solved the problem of where to fit the clergy into the social fabric; they were either nobles or commoners. But what was to be done with the new urban élite? Were these wealthy and powerful families mere bourgeois, after all, or was some credence to be accorded to their own claims of being noble in some fashion?

This was not an idle question. The families that were achieving control over city government claimed a number of privileges, including tax exemption. Where such claims were successful, especially in France and in Castile, the removal of the wealthiest families from the municipal tax rolls put an unbearable strain on public treasuries already weighted down by the demands of kings and by the needs of the poor. This is not to say that the pretensions of *rentier* families were simply geared to tax evasion. Having achieved power in their native cities, such families were turning to the far greater arena of national politics. They sought office as magistrates and treasury officials, they acquired benefices in the Church and preferment at Court. For such purposes they needed to shed the humble image of the bourgeois. They competed with the nobility for the highest positions in the realm. They became bishops, abbots, ministers of state. With the complicity of kings, who needed their capital and their expertise, these ex-bourgeois achieved a new status in a number of ways, including outright purchase of patents of nobility.

The standard test of nobility, by the late sixteenth century, was the demonstration that a family had lived nobly—that is, without working—for three generations. This standard was easily met by the members of urban élites, but it did not satisfy the feudal nobility, from whose perspective nobility was an inherited quality residing in the blood and tested on the battlefield. A standing quarrel was instituted between those who claimed that one could not become noble and those who stuck to the minimum standard of three generations away from commerce. A compromise of sorts was worked out by lawyers who represented the interests of the new class. They groped for new definitions. They spoke of a Fourth Estate, of an urban nobility, inferior to the true nobility in some ways, but legally entitled to comparable privileges.

Such a position may have seemed reasonable, but nothing could dispel the profound enmity incurred by the new class from all sides. Mocked for their pretensions by courtiers, *rentiers* masquerading as noblemen were also attacked by ordinary bourgeois, who viewed them as traitors, and by peasants who were in debt to them. We shall have occasion to observe the convergence of these grievances in times of civil war and popular rebellion. For the moment, let us ask what happened to these families when they left commerce behind and embarked on a long-term strategy of usurping noble status. Having cut themselves off from the bourgeois, did they join the nobility in anything but name?

There are two ways of approaching this question. The first is to ask whether the new men married into the old nobility, the second is to ask whether they adopted the old nobility's values. On both counts, given the fragmentary evidence assembled so far, it seems prudent to answer that the new class kept largely to itself. The urban élite allied itself with the old nobility, it would seem, only exceptionally. A very detailed study of one city shows an endogamy rate of 95 percent for the élite. The rich, officeholding, university-educated *rentiers* contracted marriage alliances with their own kind, avoiding alliances with the lesser bourgeoisie and shunning the nobility as well. The second question cannot be answered by tabulating documents such as marriage contracts, it requires more tentative assessments. The grandson of a fish merchant, dressed in velvet and silk, equipped with a lavishly furnished town house and a fine country estate, slipping easily into the king's company, ready to draw his sword when accused of being a disguised bourgeois—such a man would seem noble enough, yet contemporaries were aware of the nuances, even when the man in question was a powerful bishop or royal official. A case in point is the embarrassing scene recorded by the lawyer Louvet.

The event in question was a banquet given by the bishop of Angers to honor a visiting prince. The bishop, Guillaume Ruzé, was a man of great eminence, whose family had left commerce behind a long time ago. The Ruzés were officeholders, they owned great estates, and they had influence at court. Guillaume Ruzé stood in his episcopal palace, ready to greet the Duke of Anjou and his retinue. He surveyed the tables in the grand hall, loaded down with exquisite wines and sumptuous meats. When the duke's gentlemen arrived, they "pretended to quarrel with each other" and, under that pretext, they began to throw things at one another, "first napkins, then dishes, silver and glass, breaking windows and furniture." This puerile demonstration, reminiscent of a school cafeteria riot, was no accident. As some of the gentlemen present were to explain, the cause of the riot was that they thought it "unsuitable for a bishop who was a man of low condition, to have the audacity to wish to give dinner to a duke of Anjou."[6]

This kind of resentment was typical of the nobility's attitude toward the new class. In word, in deed, in published pamphlets, spokesmen for the old nobility deplored the rise of the new men to power, describing them as "a fourth body politic which ruins the three others."

"Let all these people be stripped of their rank" urged a French pamphleteer in 1614, calling on the government to get rid of this "bewildering quantity of officials." For good measure, "those who have their wives called ladies, although they are not descended from good and ancient houses, must be forbidden to do so, on pain of corporal punishment."[7] These complaints achieved very little. The old nobility was already secretly decimated, especially in France and in Spain, where the profitable complicities linking the royal treasury to officeholding *rentiers* had assumed enormous proportions. As a respected Burgundian writer put it, in 1589, "most of the noble houses are in the hands of new lords who have entered through marriage, inheritance or purchase in the last sixty years or so."[8]

Already in the early years of the sixteenth century, no one could be too sure of the authentic nobility of men who wore bishops' robes and of others who played the part of lords on their newly purchased estates. Consider the solemn event which occurred in the city of Meaux, near Paris, on March 19, 1516. The newly appointed bishop of Meaux was about to enter the city, to take possession of his diocese. He was an eminent personage. Already endowed with another bishopric and in possession of the abbey of St. Germain des Près, one of the richest in the kingdom, the new bishop now called upon his principal vassals to carry him ritually into the city, as ancient custom dictated. At once, objections were raised. One of those who objected most vociferously was the lord of Villemareuil. As it happens, this *seigneur's* real name was Abel de Buz, and his immediate ancestors had been bourgeois of Meaux. The bishop himself, Guillaume Briçonnet, was the grandson of a merchant and moneylender.[9]

There was no effective defense against the ambition of the new class. Occasionally, a Ruzé or a Briçonnet could be embarrassed. From time to time, pressure could be brought to bear on the royal government, forcing it to go through the motions of checking the credentials of those who claimed noble status. The king's ministers, secretaries, and advisers themselves, however, were invariably men like Briçonnet or Ruzé. To contest honors and privileges was futile. The underlying reality was clear: wealth and power were in new hands. Only the greatest noble families, safe in their possession of huge estates and close to the king's favor, were in a position to hold on to their power. Ordinary country nobles could only watch from the sidelines as the grandsons of merchants swallowed up fiefs and reached influence at court.

Was this development significant or not? No one doubts the strength of the urban élites. Their successes were achieved earlier in Tuscany than in Bavaria, their strength manifested itself in somewhat different ways in England, in the Low Countries, in Catalonia—but the general trend is clear enough. How should it be interpreted? Some historians view the partial displacement of the old nobility as something unremarkable, a mere replenishment of the ruling aristocracy's ranks. In their view, the European aristocracy had always been replenished from below and newcomers to noble status simply joined the aristocracy, blending in, becoming noble. Thus nothing changed. European society remained "feudal" until the French Revolution of 1789 suddenly changed everything.

I take a rather different view. It is perfectly possible that some families of bourgeois origin embraced the noble life wholeheartedly and that they were accepted, in time, as equals by noblemen of ancient extraction. On the other hand, we do know that marriage alliances with the old nobility were the exception rather than the rule. And we also know, in the French case, at any rate, which has been the most meticulously studied, that great dynasties of *rentiers* maintained a way of life which was their own and which remained distinct from the way of life of the old nobility.

The most obvious distinguishing mark of the new class was its connection with officeholding. The two indispensable requirements for would-be-officeholders were capital and education. Judgeships and treasury positions were sold to the highest bidder—and the sums involved were considerable. A law degree was another requirement for most significant offices. Taken together, the cost of purchasing office and the need to have a law degree created a virtual monopoly of office holding for the new class. Few country noblemen had access to the necessary capital and even fewer would have been willing to subject themselves to ten, fifteen, or even twenty years of schooling. It was schooling that turned the sons of merchants into eventual *rentiers* and officeholders. Nothing is more revealing about the goals of urban élites than was their invention of a new kind of schooling. Here, again, the French case is far better known than any other, although it is clear that German, Spanish, or English schools served their own urban élites in much the same way.

Schools of some kind had been an integral part of French city life at least since the fourteenth century. Supplementing older schools operated by cathedral chapters and monasteries, there were newer municipal grammar schools designed to teach reading, writing, arithmetic, and a little Latin to the sons, and even, on occasion, to the daughters, of merchants and artisans. Such schools offered only a rudimentary education. The teaching was usually done by a single master in rented premises. City councils were in the habit of granting small subsidies to such masters, to supplement the income they received from tuition fees. The wealthiest bourgeois were obliged to send their sons off to a university town, at great expense, if they desired the kind of advanced training that was a prerequisite for attending university lectures in law, theology, or medicine.

All this was to change very quickly in the early sixteenth century, when the possession of a law degree became indispensable for exercising even modest administrative functions at the local level. The older methods for preparing boys for a legal career were declared hopelessly inefficient. Every city of any consequence set about creating its own *collegium*, a demanding Latin school. Budgets were allocated for this purpose from public funds, private endowments were added, new standards were set for testing the competence of teachers, new buildings constructed to house the new schools. Instead of a single master, haphazardly recruited, the new *collegia* hired staffs of three, four, or five masters, all university graduates. An orderly system of classes was devised, each with its own master, its own room, its own curriculum. It was now possible for the sons of bourgeois to enter the public *collegium* at an early age, usually five, six, or seven, and to start learning Latin and even Greek efficiently enough so that they could go on to study law in their late teens.

These municipal schools were operated with public funds, they were usually tuition-free and open to all the sons of local residents, but they served, primarily, the sons of the local élite, since ordinary merchants and artisans had little use for higher learning. The needs of ordinary citizens were of a different sort. Their children could profit from some instruction in reading, writing, and arithmetic before they were old enough to enter an apprenticeship. Only the local *rentiers* were committed, wholeheartedly, to the *collegium* where their sons would learn Latin, Greek, poetry, rhetoric, and philosophy, unpractical subjects useful mainly to boys who had some expectation of rising in the world.

The new schools proved to be successful and permanent institutions because they served an indispensable function. The sons of *rentiers* had no use for apprenticeships in workshops or counting houses. They were being prepared for a life of leisure. Leisure was not to be confused with idleness. At an age when other children played in the streets or trailed their mothers in the kitchen, the boys from the best families were swallowed up each morning at 6 o'clock behind the sinister oak doors of the *collegium*. Their day was regimented according to a strict plan set down in city hall. Even after the last bell had sounded, there was homework awaiting them. After several years of this régime they were linked to their classmates and to their teachers in a solidarity which excluded the children of ordinary people from whom they were increasingly separated by their newly learned habits of thought and even by the language they used. Even if they did not all learn to discourse in fluent Latin, they did learn to speak and write good French, the language of Paris, the language of officialdom, the language of power—while other children continued to express themselves in the local dialect whose use was prohibited in the *collegium.*

Graduates of the municipal schools went on to Paris, to Orléans, Toulouse, Valence, or Bourges, to study law—occasionally medicine or theology as well. They made lasting friendships with young men of their own class, they learned to speak disparagingly of merchants and to hold frivolous and ignorant noblemen in contempt. Eventually, they married the daughters of other educated *rentiers.* Their careers took them away from their native cities.

In this way, the leading families of many cities tended to divorce their own interests from those of the bourgeois communes which they had served and led in the past. From the sixteenth century onwards, cities which had once taken pride in producing their own leadership lost much of their autonomy to royal administrators. At the same time, the partial exodus of the *rentiers* sapped the strength of local culture. The great municipal schools, having served their purpose, were eventually allowed to fall into decay. Soon there was to be "no civilization outside of Paris"— or London, or Madrid.[10] The concentration of wealth and culture in an élite, which sought out capital cities as fervently as moths seek light, led both to the notion of a capital and to that of provincial backwaters. The flight of the urban élite from commerce and local leadership was not without its compensations, however. These *letrados,* these gentlemen of a new sort, were the architects of modern culture and of the modern state.

V

THE PRIVILEGED ESTATES

That the richest merchants focused their ambition, single-mindedly, obsessively, on the acquisition of noble status is entirely understandable. From the sixteenth century onward, when regular royal taxation was becoming a fact of life, nothing could be more valuable than to find a way of reaching tax exemption. In most of Europe, tax exemption was granted to the two privileged estates, the clergy and the nobility. This privilege was justified by references to a mythical division of labor. Priests prayed and sacrificed worldly pleasures for the sake of everyone's salvation. Noblemen fought wars at great personal expense, sacrificing their lives to ensure the security of the realm. It was only natural, went the argument, that the sacrifices incurred by priests and noblemen should be suitably rewarded. Peasants, merchants, and artisans were expected to do their share by assuring the livelihood of lords and bishops—and by paying taxes.

I doubt that many taxpayers could be found who were foolish enough to swallow this argument. Against the taxes imposed by bishops, there had always been complaints. It was not easy to persuade even illiterate peasants of the special merits of priests. Even as early as the fourteenth century, such peasants were capable of saying that "the priests and the clergy, because they are wicked, extort and receive from the people the first-fruits and the tithes of products for which they have not done the smallest stroke of work." Hard pressed by the bishops' tax collectors, peasants were not necessarily in awe of ecclesiastical oppressors. On one of the rare occasions when a lucky documentary find gives us the opportunity to hear peasants talking, their conversation can hardly be considered edifying in this respect.

"We're going to have to pay the bishop's tax on new born lambs," says one of five peasants sitting under the elm tree in the village square, in the year 1320.

"Don't let's pay anything," answers another. "Let us rather find one hundred *livres* to pay two men to kill the bishop."

"I'll willingly pay my share," replies a third man. "Money could not be better spent."[1]

Resistance to Church taxation was chronic. Rebellion against royal taxation was common. Protests against new taxes usually singled out the unfairness of the assessments, which fell most heavily on peasants and artisans, leaving the clergy and nobility unscathed. The mass of the population could not escape taxation. Killing tax collectors—or setting fire, occasionally, to a nobleman's mansion—was not much help. Grievances and petitions were sent to court, without result. Always, in the end, order was restored by military force. Guns were the ultimate argument resorted to by kings in defense of privilege.

Although, in the normal course of events, the privileged orders maintained their domination in other ways, violence was ever present. Rural noblemen, accompanied by bands of armed retainers, terrorized entire counties. When such local tyrants became a clear threat to public order, their activities came to the attention of royal officials—as in the case of the Breton gentleman who went about armed with a gun and enjoyed shooting at passersby, "to give them a good scare." The same man used to frequent public auctions, beating up anyone who dared to outbid him. His servants were positioned along the highways, begging travelers for handouts and attacking them if they refused. Peasants who stood up to this petty monster were forced to drink in taverns until they could not see straight, at which point they were arrested and held until they paid him off. Even in the cities, it was not unusual to find bands of young gentlemen, drunk, armed and backed up by their servants, attacking the bourgeois night watch. And much of this violence went unpunished, since it was not easy to convict a nobleman.[2]

Acts of violence were not simply caused by youthful exuberance or by drunkenness. Violence, after all, was part of a nobleman's upbringing. He was destined to fight. He was taught to use sword and pistol. It was, indeed, his special privilege to bear arms and he carried a weapon at all times. In spite of frequent attempts to restrict the passion for dueling, gentlemen killed and wounded each other in large numbers every year. Such encounters bore little resemblance to the theatrical duels imagined by historical novelists and film directors.

"Surprise ambushes, attacks from the rear, onslaughts by overwhelming numbers were all legitimate tactics in the sixteenth century, and brought no disrepute upon the organizer," writes Lawrence Stone, citing the occasion on which Edward Windham was attacked in London's Fleet Street, in broad daylight, by twenty-five of Lord Rich's retainers, while His Lordship urged the men on with cries of "Draw, villains, draw," "Cut off his legs" and "Kill him!"[3]

The threat of violence was one of several means available to the privileged estates for maintaining their dominance over commoners. The princes of the Church were indistinguishable from secular lords in this respect. Popes and bishops, armed to the hilt, led armies to battle and knew how to fill entire provinces with terror. Still, all in all, the threat of force may be seen as a marginal tactic, hardly the mainstay of the aristocratic régime. It surfaced in times of trouble, when law and order had broken down and insurrection was in the air. At such times, the fear of armed reprisal by the nobility created terror among peasants and townsmen. In ordinary times, the privileged estates had no need to resort to arms: they had the law on their side, and they possessed immense wealth and influence.

The wealth of the privileged estates rested on the possession of land. Although the nobility rarely accounted for more than 2 percent of the population, this small group claimed ownership, through inheritance, purchase, or royal gift, of close to half the important fiefs in some regions.

Let us be more precise. It is not the nobility as a whole—nor the clergy as a whole—that was rich. Within both groups, there were large numbers of men and women who were privileged by virtue of their status, but whose income was entirely negligible. Parish priests and monks were certainly not rich. Their income is hardly distinguishable, in many instances, from the income of ordinary peasants. Within the nobility, there were many families—in Brittany a good half—who must be described as poor. At best, only a third of the Breton nobility can be described as rich.[4]

The impoverished nobleman was far more typical of his estate than was the rich lord. Most French or Spanish country gentlemen could point only to their family name, to their right to bear arms, to their tax exemptions as marks of distinction. In the region of Beauvais, Professor Goubert estimates that a good third of the country nobility were paupers. Crippled by debts, limping along on an income that would not have sufficed to maintain a country priest, those families could not have paid taxes had they been subjected to them. A typical document, among those cited by Goubert, is a barely literate appeal written by the wife of a country gentleman: "If you want to take the trouble to send someone here, you will see that I am not lying to you. The house is in ruin, we are in despair, soon we will have to go begging."[5]

If we seek to define the aristocracy as an élite combining privileges, wealth, and power, we will be wasting our time counting indigent noblemen. Stripped of their lands long ago by enterprising bourgeois, indebted, powerless, they could not even afford to answer the king's call for military service. Within the clergy, the mass of village priests was composed of peasants who had neither the revenue nor the education that would permit them to aspire to membership in a privileged élite, in anything but name. They were priests, they were shown a modest level of respect in the locality—as were the impoverished, rustic noblemen who lacked pistols and horses. Neither of these groups could seriously lay claim to the superior status ascribed to the privileged estates in official theory. It was not enough to be descended from knightly lineages, not enough to have been ordained. Without wealth, without influence, no gentleman could hope to retain anything but shadowy, vestigial remains of the powers associated with nobility. And no priest, however worthy, could hope to rise in the clerical hierarchy if he lacked wealth and influence.

If we discount most of the country gentlemen who owned no estates, who were not known at court, who could not keep up appearances—then we are left with a very small aristocracy. The same is true of the clergy. Discount the country parish priests and vicars, the monks and nuns of common origin, the salaried Protestant ministers—and what is left is a very small élite of bishops, abbots, and priors who owe their benefices to family wealth. This is the true aristocracy. It is an unimaginably narrow élite, immensely rich and immensely powerful. In the kingdom of France, rough estimates of the relative proportions of nobles, clergy, peasants, and bourgeois provide something like this: 85 percent peasants, 13 percent bourgeois and artisans, 1 percent nobles, 0.5 percent clergy. Take away the clerical proletariat, prune the nobility of its embarrassing rustics, and you reach the conclusion that fewer than 0.5 percent of the population disposed of most of the wealth and power.[6]

Land was the chief source of the aristocracy's wealth. But what does that mean, exactly? The landholding *seigneurs* of Western Europe are not to be confused with the magnates of East Prussia or the plantation owners of the New World. They did not rule over vast, newly conquered domains. They did not dispose freely of the entire crop grown on their lands, nor could they treat their tenants as if they were slaves or serfs.

When Professor Meyer concludes that 40 percent of the important

Breton *seigneuries* belonged to the nobility, this means that rich noblemen were the *seigneurs* in a large proportion of Breton villages—while other villages owed allegiance to ecclesiastical lords, to bourgeois, and to lesser nobles. Most villages had their lords, their *seigneurs*—lay or ecclesiastical, noble or not. The possession of seigneurial rights, however, must not be confused with outright ownership, nor were such rights necessarily very profitable. Their enforcement varied from county to county. Significant in some places, they were rather symbolic in others.

Seigneurial rights fell into two categories: income from the *demesne* and income from fees collected from all village households within the *seigneur's* jurisdiction. Both of these categories of seigneurial income had been pared down since the fifteenth century. The *demesne* was that portion of the *seigneurie* which belonged directly to the *seigneur*. Sizeable at one time, the *demesne* portion was shrinking and what was left of it was not as profitable as it might have been. Before the fourteenth century, a servile peasantry had been under the obligation of working on the lord's lands. These labor services evaporated in time. In the absence of free labor, *demesne* farming had become an expensive proposition for the lords, most of whom had little interest in farming anyway. Shying away from the cost and complexity of running their own agricultural enterprises with hired labor, most lords were absentees who leased the *demesne* to local farmers who knew how to reap most of the benefits from this arrangement.

Fees collected from individual village households were usually fixed amounts whose real value diminished with inflation, so that seigneurial rights of this kind ceased being of consequence in the course of the sixteenth century. Both *demesne* farming from a distance and the collection of head taxes may be considered archaic and inefficient sorts of income. Lords who depended on nothing else were likely to suffer from what we would describe as severe cash flow problems. Hence we must not be too impressed by the lists of *seigneuries* attached to a noble name. An aristocratic family could draw much prestige from the possession of seigneurial rights—and yet find itself deeply in debt.

To turn a significant profit from landed income, it was necessary to look beyond feudal rights. The sale of timber was profitable. Raising cattle and sheep on a large scale was profitable. Lending money to peasants was profitable. Although lords could be found who were willing to turn to these kinds of investments, on the whole the older aristocratic families were slow to accept new ways. Aristocratic families that prospered were more likely to belong to the newer urban élite than to old feudal lineages.

This proposition is well illustrated even in a region like Brittany where the nobility is thought to have been exceptionally numerous and influential. In this province, some 6,000 families claimed noble status in the seventeenth century, out of a total population which may have approached two million persons. When a royal commission demanded proof of nobility from those who claimed tax exemption on such grounds, some 2,000 families failed the test, even though the standards applied were hardly rigorous.[7] Of those families whose privileges stood confirmed, the majority had little in the way of land or other income. Most of the wealth and most of the *seigneuries* were concentrated in the hands of some 200 families associated with officeholding in the Breton *parlement*, the supreme court of the province. Almost all of these families were of bourgeois origin. Having shifted their capital from commerce to land and office since the late fifteenth century, these families passed the tests applied by the royal commission in 1668 with flying colors. To satisfy such commissions it was sufficient to prove that the family had "lived nobly" for three generations, or that noble status had been granted more recently by royal letters patent or through the exercise of a royal office for a specified number of years. Secure in their possession of expensive offices and vast lands, the *parlementaire* élite successfully claimed nobility in 1668, even though most of the families concerned had bought their way into office in the course of the sixteenth and seventeenth centuries. After the commission closed its books, the pretensions of the officeholders rose even higher. Open to wealthy bourgeois before 1668, the *parlements* now closed ranks, claiming that, henceforth, "no one would be accepted . . . unless he was well-born."[8]

New élites had constituted themselves everywhere in Western Europe since the early years of the sixteenth century, replacing feudal families in the possession of seigneurial rights, establishing their own claim to nobility, and closing ranks against the next wave of usurpers. Nevertheless, there was still room for new generations of aspirants to fiscal privilege. The high ground occupied by presidents in the French *parlements*—or by the English and Castilian titular aristocracy—was no longer within reach of newcomers. The inflation of honors that had been the hallmark of an earlier period slowed down at the highest levels. The time was past when a king of England dubbed 46 knights, all at once, before breakfast.[9] But there never was a time when money could not buy the appearance of nobility and the privileges this implied.

The aristocratic élite, in possession of land and royal favor for at least three generations, made up a miniscule fraction of the population. At the same time very large numbers of people claimed privilege in some form.

Take a provincial capital like Dijon, a city of some 30,000 in 1753. The number of households exempt from taxation was huge. Only a few dozen families belonged to the aristocracy of the *parlement,* but fully 2,542 persons and heads of household were privileged, nevertheless. Of these, members of the clergy accounted for close to 1,000, but an almost equal number of privileged households was made up of ordinary people—of merchants and tavernkeepers rich enough to pay the substantial sums required to have themselves declared tax exempt by virtue of a purchased office. There were bakers "by appointment to His Highness," there were "sworn inspectors of hats." Offices of "sworn inspectors of pigs" and "sworn town criers at funerals" were sold to the highest bidder. There was even a "crow catcher of the royal hunt," an ennobling office sold to the merchant Thibault Carrelet, on the condition that he give up his commercial activities. Military offices also belonged to the imaginative category of titles whose sole purpose was to achieve tax exemption. In 1699, among the 10 Dijon musketeers, privileged by virtue of their military office, there were two tavernkeepers, two bakers, and a shoemaker.[10]

The reality of privilege, by the seventeenth century, had virtually no connection at all with the medieval vision of an aristocracy of warriors whose qualities were said to be inherited, from father to son. Of those medieval knights, precious few still had descendants in possession of their ancestral fiefs in the sixteenth century. While the actual personnel of the medieval warrior caste was gone forever—the families having died out or lost their seigneurial rights—the trappings of chivalry, constantly reinterpreted, remained in place, secured by a steady flow of edicts from the royal palaces. Coats of arms were fabricated at short notice, for a price, by specialists in heraldry. The palaces and country houses of Europe were filled with phony dukes and marquises who asserted the antiquity of their privileges, which they did not hesitate to trace back to ancient Rome or even ancient Troy.

Newcomers to noble status, whether they had bought their fiefs in 1500 or in 1600, knew how to keep up appearances. They dressed the part. They built elaborate country houses. They maintained large numbers of retainers. They were presented at court. Their claims might arouse the suspicion of a handful of noblemen of older vintage, the king himself might laugh, privately, at their pretensions, but in public, as they made their way in silk-lined coaches toward masked balls and other expensive entertainments, who could deny their eminence?

Were they not received at court? Were they not lords among their peasants? Were they not set apart from commoners by their expensive wigs, their fashionable clothes, their perfumed gloves, the jeweled swords which hung from their belts? Participants in a ballet of deference, the noblemen and would-be noblemen of the seventeenth and eighteenth centuries were constantly removing and replacing their wide-brimmed hats, acknowledging the superior rank of a duke or president, receiving the homage of their own presumed inferiors. Bowing and scraping, insisting on their prerogative to remain seated or to keep their hats on, attended by servants and pushing their way into the place they felt entitled to on public occasions, hordes of men and women insisted on their various and conflicting positions in the world of privilege. They came to blows, at church, over the right to be seated in the front benches. "They are like pigs," wrote a country priest. "Like pigs, they tear each other up. They have nothing but contempt for each other, they think that they can add weight to their own reputation by accusing others of being of more recent nobility."[11] Since privilege was largely a matter of wealth and of appearances, it is not surprising that appearances mattered so much. Kings set the tone, establishing elaborate hierarchies at court. At the royal palace in Versailles, thousands of courtiers lived in fear of committing breaches of etiquette, clinging to bewildering distinctions of rank. It was bad manners to knock at a door in Versailles. The proper way was to scratch at the door with the little finger of the left hand. If the servant of a social superior brought you a message, you had to receive him standing and bareheaded. If you encountered the royal dinner on its way from the kitchens to the table, you were obliged "to bow as to the King himself, sweeping the ground with your hat and saying, in a low, reverent, but distinct voice: 'The King's dinner.'" Who could sit down, in the presence of whom, and on what, was a vexing problem at court. Two prominent people could not meet without verifying the seating arrangements in advance. A fifteen-year-old duchess, elevated by her recent marriage to a rank which made her superior to her own mother, has a screaming fit when the usher on duty throws open both leaves of the door as her mother enters the room. As her social inferior, the mother was entitled only to one half of the door being opened for her.[12]

The mania for precedence spread from the royal courts to the streets of provincial cities. At the theater, in the seaport of Brest, in 1760, Madame de Kerlorz is saving the seat next to her. A ship's captain insists on taking it, in spite of the lady's protestations. A heated argument ensues.

"You are failing to show the respect due to a woman of quality, Monsieur," says the lady. "If my husband were here . . ."

"I couldn't care less about your husband, your father, your brother and the whole family," replies the captain.

"We do have masters, Monsieur," says the lady.

"I acknowledge no masters," replies the captain, who seems to have been an unusually outspoken man.[13]

A more common response from someone reprimanded for overstepping the privileges of his rank is the kind of apology elicited, in Dijon, from a man who failed to step aside when a president came his way in the street: he explained that he had failed to recognize the president's quality, because he was dreadfully shortsighted.[14]

The "quality" of a person was constantly debated, since few families were in a position to prove their descent from medieval knights. Officially, the "quality" of a noble person resided in his blood. In reality, it had been constructed out of paper: forged genealogies, royal letters patent, portfolios of *rentes,* records of seigneurial possessions, old wills, and marriage contracts—it was in this arsenal of family papers, locked away in heavy chests and coffers, that a family's claim to privilege rested.[15]

The chief difference between those whose nobility went uncontested and those whose nobility was less esteemed was the wealth and power that surrounded great lords, even those whose elevation to royal favor was of recent origin. Between the successful baker who bought a minor office and the wealthy landowner who could afford a seat in the House of Lords, the difference was largely a matter of time. Contemporaries ridiculed men who rose to honors overnight. They reserved their admiration for families whose ascent followed a more discreet and less hasty schedule, leading from commerce to landownership, to judicious marriage alliances and proper connections among the more established gentry, to be crowned, eventually, by influence at court and a title paid for in cash.

An English baron's title could be bought for 10,000 pounds in 1616. The House of Lords, which represented the absolute top of the social pyramid in England, was constantly penetrated by new men who paid for the privilege. Even in the sixteenth century, when the English peerage had been limited to some 50 or 60 families, there were plenty of new men invested with the honor. Under James I, the creation of peers accelerated; in the course of 13 years, their number rose from 81 to 126. The King's favorite, the Duke of Buckingham, scandalized his contemporaries with his nonchalant sale of titles. Since the Spanish, French, or Swedish courts showed themselves just as ready to create dukes and barons for a price, the English inflation of honors can hardly be attributed to the exceptional greed of a single monarch and of his favorites. All European courts participated in this trend. Everywhere, nobility was for sale. Wealthy families simply could not find another way of establishing their prestige.

Short of being able to prove their genealogical link to an earlier aristocracy, they sought confirmation of their status from kings who were the fount of privilege.

Seeking recognition on the battlefield, as had been the custom of an earlier age, was not a practical option. The age of knighthood was past. Chivalry survived only as a social convention. Medieval barons did have a military rôle to play. Trained and equipped to fight in ways not open to commoners, they had dominated battlefields with their armored cavalry charges and they had furnished manpower by bringing their tenants, relatives, and servants to serve in the king's wars. In the early years of the sixteenth century, the armed nobility still supplied an important proportion of the king's soldiers. The rapid development of firearms and the monstrous growth of armies put an end to the nobility's special position in times of war. Medieval battles had been little more than multiple duels, engaging a few hundred armed knights and their followers. The new warfare of the sixteenth century put tens of thousands in the field. In the mass of musketeers, gunners, and pikemen, the knight lost his special place. Wars became long-drawn-out campaigns, involving large numbers of professional soldiers in the king's service. Supported by field artillery, equipped and paid by the royal treasury, the armies of the sixteenth and seventeenth centuries offered few opportunities for the nobility as a whole. Discouraged from building up private armies, the nobility depended on the king's favor for military commands. Courage, recklessness, and skill at sword play were of little use now, when war ceased being a sport. It was a business now, of very large proportions, requiring vast capital outlays and employing hundreds of thousands. Recruiting mercenaries, arranging for supplies of artillery and ammunition was the province of financiers, not of well-born young men seeking glory. In war as in peace, only royal favor could promote the careers of noblemen.

Although important commands were given to courtiers, most military officers bought their commissions. The transformation of the European aristocracies weakened the special link still claimed between nobility and military service. Although aristocrats still maintained that they owed their privileges to their service in time of war, commoners knew well enough that things had changed. "Our noblemen are not soldiers" protested the commoners of Dauphiné, as they attacked the privileges of the local aristocracy.[16]

And they were right, of course. A few hundred courtiers following the king to war hardly established the claims to privilege of a French nobility that might well have included 200,000 persons. Neither the Breton aristocracy nor the nobility of the Beauvaisis sought out military service. The truly rich landowners and officials saw no advantage to be gained in military careers. As for the mass of the lesser nobility, they could not afford to go to war.

In this respect, as in so many others, the meaning of nobility was changing fast. On the face of it, European society remained imbued with aristocratic values. Official acts and official propaganda stressed the aristocratic, hierarchical, and immutable order of society. Such privileges as the wearing of silk hose or the carrying of firearms were officially reserved to the well-born. An English royal proclamation of 1600 draws attention, in this connection, to the "indecent and disorderly confusion among all sorts and degrees of men—every mean and base person taking to himself that which belongeth to men of the best sort and condition."

An open challenge to the notion of rank could be costly, on occasion, as in the case of Thomas Bennett, who was fined 2,000 pounds by the Star Chamber, in 1637, for telling the Earl of Marlborough that he was as good a gentleman as His Lordship. And yet, as Professor Stone reminds us, such measures, designed to freeze the social structure, were introduced "at a time when, in fact, families were moving up and down in the social and economic scale at a faster rate than at any time before the nineteenth and twentieth centuries." Indeed, "it was just this mobility which stimulated such intensive propaganda efforts." Professor Stone's comparison of the English aristocracy to "a bus or a hotel, always full, but always filled with different people,"[17] may serve as a reminder of the fluidity that marked the rise and fall of individual families, not just in England, but most everywhere in Western Europe. Well-disguised, always denied by its beneficiaries, social mobility was a fact, nevertheless—and a permanent invitation to protest, on the part of those who were left behind in the race for privilege.

VI

THE EVOLUTION OF RURAL SOCIETY

Using the example of a very ordinary village set in the midst of a depressing region, we drew some conclusions, in an earlier chapter, about the lives of peasants. Fifty watery farms in the Sologne may suffice for setting down some elementary traits common to many peasant communities, but these must not be mistaken for a full picture. The village of Sennely presents us with a thin and fuzzy image of rural life. We will now have to collect evidence from other villages, to add substance to this bare and partial outline.

Nothing is likely to change our conclusions regarding the material constraints of peasant life. Children died everywhere, in roughly the same proportions. Surplus land and food were available to peasants only in their dreams. Rare was the village that could increase its population without running the risk of famine. In other respects, however, there was considerable diversity. We may be forced to reconsider our first impression. Sennely may be an immobile village, but we shall find plenty of movement elsewhere. We may need to soften the distinction we have drawn between a static rural world and a dynamic urban one, if only because these two worlds do not ever remain truly separate.

Consider the question of the legal status of peasants. Was it appreciably different from that of city dwellers? We know that only free men were admitted to membership in the urban commune, and we speak of personal freedom and city life in the same breath. There is no denying that personal freedom came to the countryside with the help of urban pressures. Thanks to Isabelle Guérin's study of rural life in the Sologne, we need not go very far away from the familiar territory of Sennely to hear the authentic voices of serfs pressing for emancipation. Let us look at the grievances of a peasant community, as recorded in the fall of 1468.

They are more than grievances, really. The wording of the petition presented to the lords of the manor sounds like an ultimatum. The intention of the petitioners is to have all traces of their servile status removed. Speaking for the entire community, they ask that they be declared free. What, exactly, was the difference between serfs and free peasants? Would a village change in any way as a result of a legal declaration of freedom applying to its inhabitants? Would there be more land, more grain? Would the tax burden be lighter? There was no question of anything like that. Nor must we imagine a French *seigneur* of the fifteenth century as a drunken, violent tyrant. In Western Europe, lords did not whip their subjects with impunity. No, the petitioning peasants had different concerns.

What bothered them was a sense of shame. They complained of being mocked in public and called "villeins and serfs." When they went to market, they said, "no one wished to have anything to do with them" and, even more to the point, "no one was prepared to do business with them, on the ground that no agreement entered into by a serf was legally valid without the approval of his lord. And furthermore," they added, "there was worse: they could not find suitable marriage partners for their daughters, nor could they find girls willing to marry their sons . . . because of the said condition of servitude."

In 1468, even in a backward region like the Sologne, serfs were becoming an anomaly. Shunned and mocked by free peasants, our villagers explain that if they are singled out it is only because of the shame attached to servile status. They are able to point to the inhabitants of a neighboring village who had been emancipated since 1430: those people "were not being mocked and their children were able to do well, by means of advantageous marriage alliances and in other ways." As for their own children, since they could not find brides and grooms locally, "they have gone and left so that they could be free." From which statement we may deduce how loosely defined serfdom was, in practice. It seemed sufficient to leave one's native village to shed this hereditary taint. Sturdy young men and women, hard workers, at a time when labor was scarce, could leave home and find employment elsewhere, no questions asked. For that matter, their parents now declared themselves willing to follow suit. If they were not given their freedom, they said, "they were determined to go and live somewhere else where they could be free—they and their descendants."

Faced with this threat, the lords gave in. After long negotiating sessions conducted by a delegation of villagers, agreement was reached on November 11 of that year. The serfs were declared *"bourgeois,"* in exchange for a lump sum payment of 200 *écus.* Otherwise, life would go on as before. Each year, on the day of St. Michael's feast, every household would owe 5 *sols* to the lords of the manor, a small payment in no way different from the 5 *sols* they had paid as serfs.[1]

What benefits did emancipation bring, then? Were the advantages purely psychological, having to do with self-esteem? I do not think so. One of the main concerns of peasants who had been left behind in the general rush toward personal freedom was to catch up with the economic rights already achieved by the mass of the free peasantry. These included the right to make contracts without the lord's permission, the right to inherit property from a free person, the right to will their own property freely, the right to buy and sell their heritages—their farms—and, of great importance, the right to enter into a *rente* agreement with a bourgeois moneylender. A local notary pointed out, in 1497, that "persons of servile condition may not sell their *héritages,* nor may they sell *rentes,* nor can they borrow money or grain on the strength of their land as collateral."[2] In all such dealings there remained the risk of the lord declaring the transaction null and void.

A free peasant was a peasant with whom one could do business. In this sense, it is true that the pressure for emancipation was linked to urban interests. By the mid-sixteenth century there were no serfs left in the Sologne—and the phenomenon was so general in Western Europe that we would not be far off the mark in concluding that rural society ceased to be medieval in character wherever serfs were transformed into leaseholders and tenants. It is no accident that in choosing a word that would describe the status of newly emancipated peasants, notaries recording the transaction sometimes hit upon the word *"bourgeois,"* since it would be hard to define the difference in legal rights between a free peasant and a free townsman.

Small market-towns, which lacked the walls and liberties of the more important cities, blended, imperceptibly, into the countryside. No Craft fellowships, no bishops, no lawyers disturbed the placid surface of such semirural towns which I would be hard put to differentiate from large villages, were it not for the importance of weekly markets. It may be a mistake to treat urban society as if it were somehow generically, intrinsically different from rural society. These two adjoining worlds resembled each other enough so that we may speak of a common origin. The formal village community, for instance, was as ancient an institution as was the urban commune—and it served many of the same purposes. The same can be said of village religious brotherhoods. These two kinds of associations are sometimes hard to tell apart. There were villages in which the brotherhoods performed secular functions such as the upkeep of roads and wells and the exercise of police power. The village community was reasonably well defined. A year and one day of residence was the usual requirement for membership. The payment of a fee was another, fairly common, requirement when joining the community. Membership was denied to serfs and open only to taxpaying landholders. Merchants who did not own land were not admissible, nor were vagrants, hired hands, servants, and others who were neither heads of household nor taxpayers. Such distinctions could become blurred, in practice. A peasant who owns no land but is a native of the village, owns a cottage, has a wife and children, takes care of a cow belonging to a bourgeois, may be a member of the community, even though he admits that he is "a beggar in the winter." Such a man may take to the road without forfeiting his membership. On the other hand, abandoned children sent to a peasant family by urban charities, to be nursed and raised for a small fee, were not likely to become integrated into the community, should they survive. Such orphans became servants or shepherds. In their teens, they were likely to run away and try their luck elsewhere, becoming soldiers, prostitutes, beggars, or criminals. There was no permanent place in the villages for orphans without property.[3]

Property became the measure of all things as soon as servitude vanished. One of the most striking characteristics of early modern rural society was the arrangement of households in a hierarchy dominated by a small group of rich farmers. The example of Navalmoral is not untypical. This Spanish village, studied by Professor Weisser, is situated in the mountains near Toledo. Here, 9 percent of the inhabitants owned 54 percent of the land, in 1583. Twenty-two of the village's families were openly referred to as "the rich." As opposed to those *ricos*, 95 other households in this village owned no land at all—no horses either, no mules or oxen, not even garden plots. These *trabajadores* lived by hiring themselves out. In between the *ricos* and the *trabajadores*, there was a middling category of 32 landowning families which did own a team and a plough without being rich—and a further group of 28 families which owned no land but were not badly off because they owned cattle and sheep which grazed in the common pasture. Another 12 families lived in the village without being farmers: this group included a storekeeper, an innkeeper, a miller, three weavers, two meat curers, two wool dyers, a grass weaver, and a tailor. Finally, there was a group of officially recognized paupers—17 of them—who paid no taxes, had no permanent residence, could not earn a living, and depended on charity.[4]

There were, to be sure, sharp contrasts according to region, and in spite of our first assumption about the unchanging nature of rural life—there were also periods of prosperity and periods of near starvation. A Spanish mountain village in 1583 is, by definition, a poor village. For a sharp contrast, if we consider a French village such as Azereix, situated in a fertile valley and recorded in the prosperous years of the mid-eighteenth century, we may not find absolutely landless peasants, but the distinction between rich and poor peasants remains in place.

It is expressed in the familiar way: there are 49 *laboureur* households as against 123 households of *brassiers*. The *laboureurs* own 15 acres or more—and a team of draft animals. The *brassiers* do not own a team and their landholdings are inadequate.[5] Even in this most favored village at one of its most prosperous moments, there is no escaping the fundamental distinction between those whose inheritance was adequate and those who had to hire out their hands for wages in order to eat. This distinction was summed up succinctly by the sixteenth-century inhabitants of a Spanish village: *"cinco o seis vecinos ay que tienen de comer, los demás pobres,"* that is, "we have five or six households here where there is enough to eat, the rest are poor."[6]

It may be true that there had once been a time when village society came closer to resembling a community of equals. Surviving records of land distribution in the twelfth and thirteenth centuries tend to support this view, often showing individual homesteads of roughly equal size. Even in the seventeenth century, in some unfavored regions left out of the general trend, equal holdings can be found. This is true of Northumberland, for instance, a region so poor and so thinly populated that urban capitalists were not tempted by its potential for development. The rough equality still found in such marginal zones was no more than a reminder of an earlier economy. The characteristic distribution of wealth in early modern villages was profoundly uneven—and it remained that way because rich peasants married the daughters of rich peasants, while landless men, of necessity, turned to their own kind.

If equality survived at all, it was only in its grimmest form: in almost any village, the majority of the peasant families could be said to be equally poor. Distinguished from the more fortunate villagers who owned enough land to feed their families, the mass of the peasantry lived in a state of permanent insecurity. The classic analysis of their situation is to be found in Professor Goubert's study of the Beauvais region. Having established that even an *héritage* consisting of 10 acres could not suffice to provide the six or seven pounds of bread needed to feed a family of three every day, Goubert recites the stark figures of land tenure in the seventeenth century. In the village of Goincourt, 94 households out of a total of 98 have fewer than five acres. In Coudray-St. Germer, there are 95 households out of a total of 125—in Espaubourg, 125 out of 148—with fewer than 5 acres.[7]

Faced with a staggering and chronic imbalance between the grain they could call their own and the minimum needed for survival, most peasants resorted to improvisation. They rented a few extra acres to supplement their own. They hired out in the busy summer season to work on the larger farms. They cultivated their gardens intensively, selling vegetables and fruit at nearby markets. A single, skinny cow provided milk. Pigs were few, in the Beauvaisis, where they tended to compete with human beings for nourishment. Four or five chickens in the barnyard, a few sheep out to pasture with the communal herd, this was as much as the ordinary peasant family could afford. Add the meager wages earned in the winter months from spinning and weaving cloth, and the deficit could almost be made up, in a good year. In bad times, peasants could not pay their taxes. The time came, inevitably, when they had to borrow grain. These debts resulted, sooner or later, in the loss of a portion of their remaining land. Land-hungry and indebted, peasants faced the risk of losing their prized status in the community, of sinking to the level of the landless poor.

Some of the blame for the insecurity of peasant incomes can be attributed to impersonal forces, such as bad weather. Frost or hail, an excess of rain or an inordinately long dry spell—such Acts of God did, of course, recur with frightening regularity. A succession of bad harvests could destroy the delicate equilibrium of family budgets balanced on the edge of need. At such times, entire families took to the roads, digging up fern roots, stripping trees of their bark, eating carrion, turning to roadside begging and to crime. Their flight can be traced in the parish registers along their path. The children and the old people would lie down in the snow and die. They were buried in improvised trenches or in special cemeteries for the poor. The luckier refugees found temporary shelter in poorhouses maintained by towns along their passage; there they could count on a bowl of watery soup and a straw-covered floor for the night.

Natural catastrophes hounded bad lands, such as the mountainous southern edges of the French Massif Central, a reservoir of rural misery from which peasants fled, spilling over into the sunny plains of Languedoc. Much has been written about the iniquities of the weather, about the meanness of the land, and about the Malthusian effects of overpopulation. Nevertheless, it is hard to avoid the conclusion that the greater part of peasant misery was caused by human intervention. Bad harvests did force peasants into debt, but it was the rapacity of moneylenders and tax collectors that turned temporary shortages into permanent ones.

The vagaries of the weather, the limits of grain production, the number of mouths to be fed—these may be considered constant pressures. The burden of taxation, on the other hand, and the deep inroads on peasant property caused by creditors—these were flexible pressures which tended to increase without respite. Goubert's calculations for the Beauvaisis show that 20 percent of the harvest went to the tax collector and another 12 percent into the coffers of the Church, so that only 68 percent of the grain harvested could be called the peasant's own. Another 20 percent had to be set aside for seed grain and for other expenses. A peasant family faced the winter with more than half of its grain gone. When the meager reserves ran out, in the spring, there was no way out, except borrowing.

Peasant indebtedness is not easy to analyze with precision, but it is omnipresent in the archives, having settled everywhere, "as surely as the dust." To give a measure of it, Goubert singles out three households in a single village, in 1684. Rohard, whose *héritage* is estimated at 180 *livres*, owes 175 to a bourgeois from Beauvais. Decaux, worth 510 *livres*, owes 253 to various merchants and lawyers. Lenglet owes more than he is worth, including 400 to a merchant and 300 to the tax collector.[8]

The pattern of peasant indebtedness reveals the deep roots of their poverty. There are small debts—regular, annual debts owed to the smith, to the wheelwright, to the shepherd, to the schoolmaster, to the cattle dealer. A second category of debts consists of those naturally incurred by peasants who had no horses and plows of their own. They owed payments to the richer *laboureurs* for services rendered, for seed grain, too, and firewood as well. The biggest debts, however, belong to a third category: these are the sums owed to creditors from the city—merchants, lawyers, tax collectors—to whom peasants turned when the harvest failed.

Every natural disaster set off an avalanche of documents, each of them a mortal threat to peasant independence. Faced with starvation, in a bad year—or burdened by unexpected expenses such as a funeral or the death of a horse—peasants borrowed, even when they could not entertain a reasonable expectation of repaying the loan. The lenders were glad to oblige: the investment was a safe one, the law was on the side of the

lender. The day would come when overdue payments brought on fore-
closure.[9]

Of the various afflictions that terrorized the rural world, some picked
off their victims blindly, striking rich and poor alike. Frost, hail, locusts,
fevers that struck cattle—these natural disasters did not single out the
land-poor *brassier*. Human disease could be more selective, since typhoid,
influenza, and various fevers killed off the poorly nourished more frequently than the well-fed. The most insidious threat of all, however, was
the threat of dispossession—and it was highly selective. This may not be
self-evident. One has to accumulate data covering a period of several
hundred years, as Professor Le Roy Ladurie has done, in his classic study
of the peasants of Languedoc, to observe a clear trend in the evolution of
peasant landholding after the fifteenth century.

The trend can be summed up quickly. Where there had been many
middling-size holdings as late as 1450, there were few left by 1700. In
1460, in a village with 189 households, for instance, 62 had enough land
for their needs. Generally, there was still, in fifteenth-century Languedoc,
a reasonably even distribution of property. Rich peasants were rare—and
so were landless peasants. Half the households could still be described as
occupying a comfortable middle position. One family in four was assessed, for tax purposes, at a rate which implies an adequate standard of
living.

The deterioration of this yeomanry occurred very quickly. Where one
household in four had been financially secure in 1505, only one in nine
could still make that claim in 1539. Where half the peasants occupied
sizeable properties in 1460, only 10 percent still did in 1690. The medium-sized holding soon became an oddity. It was replaced by a large
number of tiny properties and a few large ones.

The subdivision of land into smaller and smaller holdings certainly
could not have happened without a general increase in the population.
The happy situation of fifteenth-century peasants owed much to the
ravages of the Black Death, which had thinned the ranks of the living. But
it is not enough to note the general increase in population in the sixteenth
century. There were more mouths to feed, yes, and the competition for
land grew fiercer—but this does not explain how some peasants increased
their holdings at the expense of others. The elimination of medium-sized
holdings, the growth of large ones, the creation of a mosaic of minuscule
properties, these changes were linked to a new fluidity in the real estate
market. Buying, selling, and borrowing became easier. Urban capital
played havoc with the destinies of peasants in need. The pressure to sell

parcels of land was not entirely caused by weather and demographic changes. It was caused, in part, by the new burden of taxation and by the new burden of rents paid to absentee investors.

Between 1400 and 1600, the share of the harvest handed over by tenants and sharecroppers in Languedoc increased from 25 percent to 50 percent. The impoverishment of the peasantry was linked, directly, to the activities of bourgeois who bought up land, lent money, contracted for the collection of royal, seigneurial, and clerical taxes, seized and adjudicated delinquent properties, raised rents, and depressed wages. As a result, most peasants in Languedoc had sunk to a lower standard of living by the end of the sixteenth century, even though agricultural products kept on fetching higher prices. There were profits to be made from the sale of wheat, wine, and olive oil, but they were made by urban owners, creditors, and speculators—not by those who worked the land. Farm wages lost at least a third of their real value. A mason's daily wage, in the Languedoc countryside, had been worth the equivalent of thirty pounds of bread in 1480; by 1530, it was down to 18 pounds. Women's wages became especially depressed. Paid as much as four fifths of a man's wage in 1350, a woman agricultural worker could count on no more than half of a man's wage in the sixteenth century.[10]

The contrast between a thriving agricultural economy and an impoverished peasantry was evident, especially, in the most intensively cultivated lands close to big cities, where urban capital had gone furthest in penetrating the countryside. A fine example of rich lands worked by poor people was the Lombard plain dominated by the huge city of Milan. The poverty of the Lombard peasants certainly cannot be attributed to the quality of the land, which was known as "the very Paradise and Canaan of Christendom," according to an English traveler, in the seventeenth century, who noted that "the soil here never rests." The fields were "full of trees planted by man his hande, in sutche order that they hinder not the growth of corne [grain] under them—and the vines growe agaynst them, so that a man has his bread, wyne and fewell in one field."

The productivity of the Milanese countryside was extraordinary. Irrigated by rivers and by canals, the land never stood fallow. Cereal crops alternated with grass and flax. Stall-fed cattle produced enough milk to supply the Milan markets with 100,000 pounds of cheese in a single year. Milan, with a population of 120,000, consumed enough grain to account for the production of 70,000 acres. Further quantities were exported. The pastures of the hill zone to the north could supply 27,486 head of cattle annually. Linen, silk, and wool cloth was produced in the countryside.

Paper mills, brickyards, blast furnaces, and marble quarries dotted the land.

The wealth of this Paradise, however, did not benefit the peasants, who were mostly hired hands (*brazanti*) working for wages. Peasant proprietors were rare. The process we saw at work in Languedoc reached its fullest form in Lombardy, when wages, taxes, prices, and rents were all geared to the needs of the city at the expense of an increasingly impoverished rural labor force.[11]

To be sure, the Lombard case is an extreme one. There were, after all, few metropolitan centers in Europe comparable to Milan. Most peasants were exposed to the manipulations of urban *rentiers* in less direct and brutal ways. Attenuated, delayed, cushioned by slower local economies, the weight of urban power was, nevertheless, felt everywhere, testing the resilience of ancient village solidarities.

The integrity of village communities was assaulted from all sides. The rural economy became more solidly linked to urban markets, urban capital, urban sources of employment. High-profit crops, such as wine and wool, competed with subsistence farming. English and Castilian sheep drove marginal peasants off their land. Burgundian vineyards became so valuable that investors from Dijon bought up land at a pace sufficient to transform peasant proprietors into hired hands. By the eighteenth century, according to a trustworthy estimate, three quarters of the Burgundian peasantry had been reduced to poverty.[12]

Even relatively insulated villages, such as Azereix, could not escape the trend. The village was forced to give up 44 percent of its harvest in the form of royal, seigneurial, and clerical taxes. In spite of the cohesion of this community, which opposed a common front to the demands placed upon it—in spite of prudent marriages, designed to prevent the subdivision of inheritances—the number of *brassiers* kept increasing, even in Azereix. By the end of the eighteenth century, three quarters of the inhabitants had been reduced to the level of hired hands. At the same time, more arable land was turned into pasture and vineyards, as the richer *laboureurs* found it to their advantage to raise cattle and produce wine for the market.

While the most visible trend was the impoverishment of the majority, a second, happier result of commerce with the city was the enrichment of a minority of *laboureurs* who learned to swim with the new current. Aided, no doubt, by sheer luck, and prepared to profit from the market economy because they already belonged to the village élite, these enterprising *laboureurs* may have gotten their start as part-time smiths, carters, or cattle dealers. Putting their experience as managers of seigneurial estates to good use, they knew how to hire farmhands for seasonal work, how to keep accounts, how to sell grain and wool in the name of absent owners. Such men were obvious choices for elected positions as tax collectors and village mayors. Their brothers and uncles became village priests, learning the intricacies of clerical taxation. As part-time merchants, lending grain and cash to lesser folk and buying up parcels of land adjacent to their own, these rich peasants were the driving force in every village. It is they who insisted on hiring schoolmasters, so that their children would learn to read, to write, and to figure.

The schoolmasters themselves often belonged to the same rural bourgeoisie which produced priests and tax collectors.[13] How effective they were in the classroom is hard to say. The fact is that a sizeable proportion of the peasantry was literate enough to sign contracts—more than half of the men in Azereix, for instance. Literacy, however defined, was certainly not an evenly shared skill. More men than women could write their names and there were times when literacy appeared to be growing—at other times it receded.[14] What is beyond doubt is that those who needed to resort to reading and writing could do so. Unusual among hired hands, literacy was taken for granted among the village notables. For them, paperwork was as critical a skill as plowing or pruning. Already set off from their fellow villagers by their greater wealth and by their acknowledged position of leadership in the community, these rural bourgeois also possessed an adequate tincture of learning.

Their houses were larger and better furnished. They owned wardrobes to match their other advantages. Even in the impoverished mountain villages studied by Professor Weisser, the households of the *ricos* were furnished with heavy oak and walnut tables and hutches. Porcelain and pottery was to be found on the shelves, and their luxurious, canopied four-poster beds were covered with lace-edged blankets. Framed paintings, mirrors, and silver crucifixes were fixed to the walls. Silk breeches, waistcoats, and fashionable hats were stored in the wardrobes. These village *ricos* could pass muster, on a Sunday's outing in Toledo. Their standard of living resembled that of Toledo shopkeepers rather than that of their neighbors in the *pueblo*.

Next door to such *rico* households, *trabajadores* lived in austere surroundings: a small chest, a few pine benches, some pictures of saints on the walls were all they could afford. As for the *pobres*, if they were lucky enough to have the use of a one-room cottage for their family, they had to manage with the bare necessities: two beds, a table, a bench. Other *pobres* owned only a single shirt, a single pair of trousers, and a coat of some sort.[15]

Rich peasants, literate and familiar with the ways of the city, encountered no real obstacles in their way if they chose to disassociate themselves from their fellow villagers and to become assimilated, gradually, into the urban bourgeoisie. It may not be possible to establish the exact proportions of such defections, but the genealogies of even the most prestigious urban families, once stripped of false pretensions, tend to lead back to distant village origins. The sons of prosperous *laboureurs,* having established residence in a nearby town, would marry the daughters of bourgeois, acquire houses and shops, and send their children to city schools. A generation later, their descendants will have become lawyers, notaries, managers of clerical estates, wholesale merchants. Some of them would continue to rise in the world to the point of running for office and joining the urban élite, especially in the fast-moving years of the early sixteenth century. The members of Frankfurt's exclusive Limpurger Society were all descended from rich peasants. The richest man in Europe, Jacob Fugger, of Augsburg, was descended from rich peasants who had established residence in the city in the fourteenth century. There were university professors, bishops, ministers of state, and chancellors of the realm separated from their peasant origins only by two generations.

If we count parcels of land and measure the revenue of peasants, we come away with the correct impression that, for most of them, the future held out few prospects of improvement. On the contrary, they could look forward to being reduced to even greater need. Rural society was changing fast—too fast, certainly, for the victims who stood by helplessly as they saw their inheritance decrease. While the fields of the richer *laboureurs* increased in size and value, the really spectacular gains were made by the absentee owners of large properties—those who owned several farms and leased them out, those who bought up parcel after parcel, over the years, put them together, enclosed them with hedges and stone walls, or bought out the local *seigneur* to farm the *demesne* lands with crews of hired laborers.

It is possible that landless peasants bore grudges against their better-off neighbors, to whom they may have lost a field or two within living memory. There is no doubt at all, however, about the target of the deepest resentments, which were reserved for outsiders, for bourgeois, noble or pseudo-noble landowners, and clerical tithe collectors—that conspiracy of absentees whose agents pressed peasants at harvest time. Driven to despair, the peasantry identified its hereditary enemy: tax collectors, money lenders, tithe contractors, lawyers, court clerks, small-town officials—all those sleek, fat personages who were so quick with pen and paper and who operated from behind the walls of the city, cloaked in the power of the law. When a bad harvest or marauding troops threatened to reduce entire provinces to misery, peasants revolted. They assembled by the thousands, drank, swore, set fires, and marched, at last, to lay siege to the cities, calling on the urban poor to join them.

VII

REBELLION

Peasant rebellions were not exceptional events. They erupted so frequently in the course of these four centuries that they may be said to have been as common in this agrarian society as factory strikes would be in the industrial world. In southwestern France alone, some 450 rebellions occurred between 1590 and 1715.[1] No region of Western Europe was exempted from this pattern of chronic violence. The fear of sedition was always present in the minds of those who ruled. It was a corrective, a salutary fear—since only the threat of insurrection could act as a check against unlimited exactions.

When reports of sedition reached officials in the cities, when church bells could be heard tolling in the countryside, summoning the men to assemble—and smoke was seen rising from burning castles—then, at last, dispatch riders were sent off to the capital, bearing the dangerous tidings.

We know of these rebellions almost entirely from reports made to government authorities by officials who watched the progress of insurrection, called for help, and, eventually, presided over the trial and execution of the mutineers—which is to say that the surviving evidence is distinctly and ferociously partisan in tone. The sheer volume of the evidence, however, is so overwhelming that it is possible to compensate, occasionally, for the built-in bias of the accounts, and to come reasonably close to an understanding of the motives of rebellious peasants.

It is not enough to say that peasants, the world over, always have good cause for rebellion. This may very well be true, but if we go out of our way to ignore the specific circumstances under which European peasants rebelled in the seventeenth century, if we lump all peasant rebellions together, whether they occur in China, in England, or in Russia—in the twelfth or in the nineteenth centuries—then we will fail to understand the difference between Western peasants and Asian ones, between medieval serfs and early modern tenant farmers. And there were differences, profound differences.

We do know, after all, that Western peasants, in time, were to achieve political power. Already in the sixteenth century, the free, property-owning peasants of Western Europe did not resemble the servile peasants of the East. In the eighteenth century, in spite of high taxes, indebted, to be sure, and filled with powerful grievances—but often literate and resourceful—the rural population of Western Europe made its weight felt in ways that were not available to peasants elsewhere. Riots and rebellions turned into effective revolutionary agitation. Peasants became citizens and they learned to form alliances with artisans and merchants.

This did not happen overnight, in the summer of 1789. For hundreds of years, men, women, and children suffered, fought, and died to defend their livelihood against the depredations of the mighty. The "army of the suffering," as the rebellious peasants of Normandy called themselves, always lost its wars. Peasant fantasies of easy triumphs were never realized. The Englishman accused of saying, in 1596, "that there would be such a rising as had not been seen in a great while," that "he would cut off all the gentlemen's heads," and that, as a result, "we shall have a merrier world shortly," was mistaken—as were the Austrian peasants, some years later, who roamed the countryside, singing these words: "The whole country must be overturned, for we peasants are now the lords, it is we who will sit in the shade, the priests must leave their cloisters, for the peasants are now the masters."[2]

They were never the masters for very long. The followers of Stefan Fadinger, who sang these verses, were massacred—and the same fate awaited rebelling peasants every time. Nevertheless, I believe that an evolution can be discerned in the character of peasant rebellions since the fourteenth century. Earlier rebellions tended to be local uprisings directed against some particularly unpopular lord—acts of vengeance made possible by the chaos that followed vendettas among warlords. When a more general uprising comes to our attention in the twelfth and thirteenth centuries, it is likely to have a religious coloration. Medieval peasants were attracted to fantastic prophecies of the sort familiar to students of Chinese rebellions. Crusades led by visionaries enlisted masses of European peasants at one time.

Later rebellions retained some mark of the older prophetic slogans, reminders of the more radical side of Christian preaching. The famous verse associated with the English rebellion of 1381 belongs to this category. "When Adam delved and Eve span, who was then the gentleman?" was the riddle heard then. Indeed, when only Adam and Eve existed, when peasant Adam plowed his land and peasant Eve sat at her spinning wheel, there could have been no gentlemen around—no landlords, no lawyers. How, then, did gentlemen come into the picture? When did they insinuate themselves into God's universe? Was there a place for them? Had not the time come to set things right back to the way they had been in the Garden of Eden, was this not God's intention?

This way of thinking remained alive for centuries, feeding the righteous anger of desperate people. The very words which had been sung by Kentish laborers marching toward London in 1381 could be heard, more than 300 years later, in a German version which served as the battle cry of other peasants in arms: *"Da Adam ackert und Eva spann, wer war damals ein Edelman?"* sang German peasants, in 1679, adding, pointedly: "Who does the nobleman think he is, setting himself up as being better than I?"

Many rebellions, in the sixteenth and seventeeth centuries, still carried an appeal to the Christian Gospel, which is not surprising, since priests were often found among the leaders of the rebels. It really mattered little whether the spiritual leadership came from evangelical radicals, as in the German peasant wars of 1525—or from Catholic village priests, the sons of peasants, joining battle against oppressive taxation, as in the case of the Barefoot Men of Normandy, in 1639.

Although they were usually persuaded that God was on their side, Western peasants, after the thirteenth century, did not, ordinarily, take up arms in order to usher in the Kingdom of God. They did not expect miracles. Their enemy was not Satan. Their ambition did not extend to the righting of all wrongs. They rarely entertained visions of a world transformed, cleansed of evil and suffering. Myth and fantasy were absent from their petitions.

Their goals were worldly, modest, and attainable—which is not to say that they did not frighten the mighty. On the contrary, vague, messianic hopes of a better world might have been easier to deflect than were the precise and legalistic demands presented by delegations from the rebel camps. Perhaps peasants lacked imagination. They swore that it was not their aim to contest the king's authority; that they were, indeed, his most loyal subjects. They proclaimed no intention of changing the social order. They did not question the privileges of the nobility. They did not wish to change the laws. They took up arms—so they said—only to uphold the laws which had been infringed, of late, by cunning lawyers, greedy landlords, unauthorized tax collectors, and foreign soldiers.

Such an interpretation of the motives of rebelling peasants may be applied only in part to the German Peasants' War of 1525. In this early and bloody confrontation, the rebels' grievances included complaints against new taxes. The economic pressures under which German peasants were suffering at the time resembled those which were to provoke later rebellions elsewhere. The components of despair, in the German lands of the 1520s, were indistinguishable from those to be found at any time in Western Europe, whenever peasants resorted to armed resistance. What was different about the German Peasants' War was that, in this particular case, social conflict happened to coincide with a religious revolution of exceptional dimensions. It was the appeal to the Gospel, lately brought into prominence by Martin Luther, that gave the German Peasants' War its especially threatening character.

In the immediate aftermath of the Lutheran triumphs, Germans from every territory and from every social level were observing the collapse of the oldest institution in their midst. With hardly any prodding, princes and cities declared their independence from the Holy See, moved only, it seemed, by the rhetoric of a Wittenberg professor. Even in conservative and tightly ruled cities, such as Nürnberg, subjects now refused to pay tithes and called for the dissolution of monasteries. It was against monasteries that riots and gatherings were directed, in the spring of 1524—the earliest manifestations of what was to become known as the Peasants' War. The rioting peasants wanted monasteries closed down, their income to be used in future in such a way that "the poor man's burden may become easier to bear."

In making such demands, the embattled peasants were participating in the general mood of euphoria that was sweeping across German lands, in the wake of Luther's call for reformation. Some of the peasants' grievances, especially those directed at clerical establishments, appeared reasonable to those of the lords, princes, and city councillors who favored reform. Support of a militant kind came from the new breed of evangelical preachers who were suddenly allowed their say without having to fear the Inquisition. Of those preachers, one of the most radical was Thomas Müntzer, the son of an artisan. He had studied theology in Leipzig and taken up his ministry, with Luther's support, in Zwickau in 1520. He was preaching in Allstedt, in March of 1524, when the disturbances began. Here he founded the "union of the elect," which was to spearhead the struggle against the "godless." Müntzer called on the princes to join him. When they turned him down, he began denouncing "godless rulers" and moved on to the key city of Mühlhausen, which, with 7,500 inhabitants and 19 dependent villages, was then the biggest city in central Germany.

It is in Mühlhausen and in its surrounding territory that the link between evangelical preaching and social revolt may be seen most clearly.

The city was experiencing social tensions of the kind one would naturally expect to find in most sixteenth-century cities. About 40 percent of the population within the walls was made up of artisans. Another 35 percent or so were farmers. Although political power was in the hands of a small élite, it seems that as many as half the citizens did participate in the political process in some way. Of the remaining population, a sizeable proportion was doing poorly. About 25 percent had incomes hovering dangerously close to what was then considered poverty. Some 10 percent were outright paupers, having no property at all. The situation was worse in the suburbs, where the proportion of paupers came close to 40 percent.

The poorer inhabitants, both within the city and in the suburbs, joined by a number of peasants and artisans who were only slightly better off, made their grievances felt in petitions to the city council. These grievances were expressed forcefully, in the name of the poor, by an ex-monk named Pfeiffer. Before Müntzer's arrival, Pfeiffer had already gotten important concessions from the ruling faction in city hall. When Müntzer reached Mühlhausen on August 15, 1524, he placed himself at the head of the party of the poor. He announced that, henceforth, his followers were to refuse to obey the authorities, stop paying rents and other dues, and demand the removal of the old clergy. Riots broke out. Müntzer's followers formed a militia, the "eternal union of God." This first confrontation led to Müntzer's banishment, but he was back in town by February 1525. In March, an "eternal council of God" was elected. The monasteries were taken over.

Müntzer's success provoked reactions among the great lords of the province. Some of them began to arm. Others hesitated. Some seemed resigned: "If it be God's Will, it may come to pass that the common man shall rule," wrote one German lord on April 14.

In the course of a few weeks, between late March and early May, peasant militias achieved control over much of the German countryside. Town after town opened its gates to the rebels. Organized as roving bands with elected leaders, the peasants, at first, demanded the removal of the old clergy. Soon, the constant appeal to the Gospel as the only source of authority was to lead to a review of all existing customs. "In the mirror of the Holy Gospel," the peasants discovered that "the common man was oppressed by injustice." Confrontations, which would have been limited to local economic grievances in other circumstances, escalated into a general crusade against the privileged. Whatever may have been customary in the past was to be reformed if it did not "conform to the Word of God."

This message poured from the printers' presses with exceptional vigor and speed. Some 527 German-language titles had been published in the five-year period preceding Luther's rise to prominence. In the five-year period following 1517, 3,113 titles were published. The key component of this flood of printed matter was a cheap pamphlet literature addressed mainly to the common man. Some 10,000 such pamphlets were printed by the year 1530. Assuming that most press runs were limited to something like 1,000 copies, this adds up to 10 million pamphlets in circulation, at a time when the total German-speaking population did not exceed 12 million.

While much of this pamphlet literature was concerned with the reform of the clergy, some of it had a revolutionary character and spoke directly to the radical peasants and artisans whose movement was acquiring the stamp of a Holy War, of a "brotherly and christian undertaking" which transcended local concerns. This was the case, notably, of the *Twelve Articles* first published in Augsburg in March of 1525 and quickly reprinted everywhere. There were 25 editions in 15 different cities of this pamphlet which spelled out the program of the Peasants' War.

From the perspective of the established authorities and their spokesmen, including Luther, the peasants were like wild beasts on the rampage. From their own point of view, the peasants were not rebellious at all. They were guided by principle—the only valid principle—that of God's justice. Their aim was to bring the world into conformity with this principle, which required that all men be brothers, all equal in the eyes of the law. "None must be more than the common man," stated the authors of the *Twelve Articles,* most likely a journeyman of Memmingen named Sebastian Lotzer and the local preacher, Christoph Schappeler. Even when they destroyed castles, as they did very efficiently, in the territories of the diocese of Bamberg, for instance, in the course of a ten-day campaign in May 1525, the armed peasants did subject themselves to the discipline of their elected leadership. Inventories of confiscated property were drawn up and the dispossessed owners were allowed to keep as much as was estimated fitting. The rest was shipped to a central location for accounting and orderly distribution, except for the food and wine found in the pantries and cellars of the once mighty.

There was a brief moment when it seemed possible that the authority of lords and city councils might collapse as quickly as had the authority of the church. But the peasants' victories proved ephemeral. Nowhere did they stay in power for more than a few weeks. The princes concentrated their troops against one peasant stronghold after another, massacring peasants by the thousands. The corpses were hardly buried when the avenging authorities set about restoring the old order by means of heavy fines. The cost of the rebellion was high: some 75,000 peasants lost their lives. The survivors were forced to pay, both for damages and for the cost of putting the rebellion down.[3]

The German Peasants' War was unusual, both because it spread to an exceptionally large area, embracing the Rhine Valley and much of central and southern Germany, and because of the rebels' program, which had risen above local grievances to question the entire social order. But other rebellions too, rebellions whose objectives were more limited, were bound to provoke fundamental fears of dispossession and bloodshed in the minds of landlords and clerics.

A case in point is the rebellion in the English Midlands, which occurred in the spring of 1607. "About the middle of this month of May," reported a contemporary observer, "a great number of common persons suddenly assembled themselves in Northhamptonshire. Others of like nature assembled themselves in Warwickshire, and some in Leicestershire. They violently cut and brake down hedges, filled up ditches, and laid open all such enclosures of commons and other grounds as they found enclosed."

Breaking down hedges to arrest the spread of enclosures was a common act of defiance on the part of farm laborers who perceived the enclosing of pasture lands for the exclusive benefit of landlords as an act of war directed at them. The rioters in the Midlands said that their revolt was not directed against the king and lawful authority; they leveled hedges, they said, "only for the reformation of those late inclosures, which made them of the poorest sorte, reddy to pyne for want."

Rebellion was always provoked by some recent action such as "those late inclosures," which ran against the peasants' view of their natural rights and threatened to dispossess them. Reacting against the new enclosures in the Midlands, "these tumultuous persons grew very strong, being in some places of men, women and children a thousand together, and at Hill Norton in Warwickshire there were three thousand, and at Cottesbich there assembled of men, women and children to the number of full five thousand."

In spite of the peasants' protestations that they merely wished to undo the new enclosures, they were seen as dangerous revolutionaries. In June of that year, after the rebellion had been crushed, with much loss of life, a parson in Northhampton spoke of the hidden terrors released in the minds of clergymen and landlords by the leveling of hedges: "They professe nothing, but to throwe downe enclosures . . . but, afterward, they will reckon for other matters," the parson assured his congregation. "They will acompt with Clergiemen," he warned. They mean "to kill up Gentlemen, and they will levell all states as they levelled banks and ditches." The parson read the peasants' demand for leveling as a sinister metaphor, a call for the leveling of "all states"—a demand for equality, for the abolition of privilege, for the eradication of all differences between commoners and gentlemen.[4]

Peasants always rebelled against some specific and recent infringement of their rights. They were often very well informed about the rights which had been lost. Their opponents liked to picture rebellious subjects as ignorant and bloodthirsty rustics, pinning contemptuous labels on the mobs they feared. Parisian publicists referred to rebelling peasants as "Jacques" and "Croquants," names which suggested ignorance and brutality. Peasants were pictured as a breed apart, to be feared by townsmen. Whenever possible, rebellious peasants were accused of heresy and of unimaginable wickedness, including sexual perversion and cannibalism. Sober analysis of the rebellions tends to show something quite different.

In the immediate background of major rebellions, there was usually some arbitrary act of government or some long-standing grievance having to do with unfair taxation. The rebellion of the Barefoot Men was a direct reaction against the imposition of a salt tax which threatened the salt workers—the barefoot men—of the Norman beaches. It was the arrival of an official suspected of carrying the new salt edict in his saddle pouch that set off the rebellion. A crowd of salt workers and wood carriers marched on the town of Avranches, where the official had just checked in, and lynched him. In the course of a few days, the Barefoot Men were organized for combat. Their leaders were educated men who published manifestos calling on Normans to defend their ancient rights, as guaranteed by the charter of 1315. The new taxes were illegal, they said, because they had been announced without being approved by local delegates. The revolt was directed against outsiders—*Horzains*—who were sent from Paris to oppress "a people languishing under tyranny." Not above reminding their readers of the fate reserved for tyrants—"Caesar and Catalina were murdered because of the abuses they were guilty of towards the people"—the Barefoot Men were careful, all the same, to define their limited goals. They did not murder or loot indiscriminately. Instead, they sent punitive expeditions against the residences of tax collectors, declared their loyalty to the king, claimed that they were upholding the law against usurpers who bent it to their profit—and called on the inhabitants of cities to join them.

This last tactic, in particular, provoked anguish in high places. The grievances of peasants were almost never purely rural grievances. When a combination of scourges at last moved peasants to take up arms, one could be sure that the urban poor were suffering under the same pressures—and that they were likely to join the peasants when it came to a confrontation. Where was the city that contained no peasants within its walls, men ready to open the gates to the armies of the suffering without? Henry Kamen writes that "those who helped gather in the harvest in the fields in July, were pacing the streets of the city in December"[5]—and this is not a mere guess, for, as we shall see, the permanent presence of large numbers of farm laborers in cities was an ordinary feature of early modern society.

These urban peasants would not be alone in making common cause with the farmers in the fields. Major rebellions responded to pressures so broad that most of the population felt them. Rebellions that may have started in the countryside soon threatened to engulf the cities as well, enlisting sympathy not only among apprentices but among master craftsmen as well, even among merchants. The Barefoot Men of Avranches were led by Jean Quetil, who passed for noble and who was not poor, by any means, being descended from a family of bourgeois lawyers and officials. He was married to the daughter of a tax collector.[6] The Norman revolt was to spread to most of the province, embracing large cities and small market towns in its wake. We cannot very well speak of rural rebellion as a distinct and separate manifestation of the blind anger of savage peasants. It would be more accurate to say that villagers, being more vulnerable, were the first to suffer and the first to revolt. They were also easier to massacre, lacking, as they did, the protection of ramparts and artillery.

A fine case study of a peasant war in all its complexity is provided by Emmanuel Le Roy Ladurie's *Carnival in Romans*.[7] The rebellion analyzed in that book contains all the ingredients found in other rebellions, with the difference that, in this particular case, the sources are so rich that it becomes possible to understand the actions of armed peasants and of their urban supporters clearly enough so that we need not resort to stereotypes as we search for explanations.

Elsewhere, mobs of armed insurgents come to our attention briefly, seen through the haze of official reports. In Normandy, in Aquitaine, in Catalonia, or in England, we hear of crowds assembling in marketplaces, we shudder at atrocities committed, we hasten toward the inevitable conclusion of a familiar tragedy. Pushed to desperation, the "croquants" have revolted against their oppressors and, in due time, they are scattered by the cavalry—their leaders bribed, tortured, executed, and banished. We have body counts of the slaughtered. We shape these into improvised explanations. We speak of class war. We reduce the dead to sociologists' categories.

The peasant wars of 1579 which took place in the Rhône Valley, near the city of Romans, in the French province of Dauphiné, are exceptional only because, for once, the protagonists step out of the shadowy world to which rural rebellions are ordinarily consigned. The peasants who fought this war do not speak to us directly—that would be asking too much. Their skirmishes, their assemblies, their grievances—these are known to us indirectly through accounts left by bourgeois.

The chief of these accounts is hostile to the peasants. It is a long anonymous memorandum attributed to Judge Guérin, the political boss of the city of Romans. A second account, written by a notary named Piémont, is surprisingly sympathetic to the rebels. These two sources can be fleshed out by a great quantity of evidence of the most diverse sort— because the Dauphiné rebellion reached the cities from the start. In the last resort, however, it is to the skill of Professor Le Roy Ladurie that we owe our understanding of this rebellion.

On the face of it, the Dauphiné rebellion could have been fitted into a standard account of a *jacquerie*. When pressed too hard, like bears baited once too often, peasants can become dangerous, we might conclude. As they turn on their tormentors, the rustic *jacques*, who do not understand the world beyond their fields, simply lose control and go on a rampage, until their fury is exhausted. Viewed in this way, rioting peasants cannot be reasoned with. There is no point in listening to their grievances, no point in rectifying abuses. The authorities understood such rebellions as diseases that must run their course and against which a good bloodletting was the only known remedy.

Since historians tend to remain the prisoners of their sources, it is not surprising that the historical literature devoted to peasant rebellions has rarely challenged official accounts. From Marx to Mousnier, peasants at war have been described as dumb brutes rising in anger against intolerable oppression.[8] It is only in recent years, as we have learned more about rural society, that our eyes have been opened to the discrepancy between the peasants we know and the shadowy brutes pictured in the official accounts of contemporaries. The peasants of Dauphiné were not a breed apart, a special, rustic race of desperate wretches out of tune with the world of cities, driven to revolt by instinctive urges, incapable of formulating a political program, tumbling headlong into confrontations that they could not win, in the name of obscure fantasies. On the contrary, these peasants were led by village notables who could read and write, who hired lawyers to represent them and who formed alliances with urban radicals. They did not hit out blindly. They seemed well informed, they knew the laws, and they understood very well who was stripping them of their rights.

When the peasants of Dauphiné took up arms in the spring of 1578, they did so to defend themselves against outlaws and soldiers who stole their cattle and endangered their lives. Although the peasants did not challenge the authority of the provincial governor, their actions could be interpreted as seditious from the start, since they acquired weapons and elected captains to lead them into battle. They established unions and leagues in which villages became associated in a common fight against dangerous *horsains*—outsiders who roamed the province with impunity, undeterred by royal garrisons stationed in the cities. The garrisons, composed of mercenary soldiers who had to be fed and supplied by the local population, constituted a threat more serious than the bandits they were supposed to keep in check. Already, in the cities of Valence, Montélimar, and Romans, there was talk of ousting the regiments. Urban leagues were forming, to put pressure on city councils, in the hope of ending the costly military presence.

In May 1578, a peasant militia drawn from several villages laid siege to an armed band of soldiers of fortune, east of Romans. The bandits surrendered. In November, the peasant leagues sent a spokesman to a meeting held in the city of Montélimar. The peasant delegate denounced the thefts and acts of violence perpetrated both by bandits and by soldiers. He called for immediate and joint action, adding that the peasant militias had already sent a delegation to the governor in Grenoble and that they asked for nothing better than to serve under his authority. Pressure mounted for vigilante action. A combined force of peasants and townsmen, under the leadership of a popular bourgeois of Montélimar, Jacques Colas, set out to destroy the headquarters of a local bandit chieftain in February 1579. Brought into being by the fear of marauding outlaws, the leagues quickly became a force to be reckoned with. Montélimar, Valence, and Romans ousted their garrisons. Vienne was to follow suit. Emboldened by their success, the leagues began to press for permanent reforms. New taxes had been announced in October 1578. Now there was talk of a tax strike and of a moratorium on the debts owed by both rural and urban communities to financiers in Lyon.

So far there had been no sign of the senseless killings we have been taught to expect when peasants rebel. No mobs were out of control, although landlords and magistrates were nervous. The leadership of the leagues was made up of men who had considerable standing in their communities. In the villages, they were rural bourgeois experienced in dealing with the authorities. Some owed their popularity to success in the games organized at carnival time. They were Princes of Youth, winners of races and other athletic contests, captains of bachelor societies. In the urban leagues, also, the leaders were far from being marginal desperadoes. Colas, the popular leader in Montélimar, was a lawyer and officeholder who had been elected Prince of Youth in his student days at the university, in Valence. Only two years before the revolt, he had been one of the deputies of the Third Estate of Dauphiné at the Estates General meeting in Blois. In the provincial capital, Grenoble, the most popular agitator in favor of the leagues was the lawyer Gamot, who spoke of Swiss freedom as he handed out little wooden trumpets similar to those used by the Swiss.

The grievances of the peasants were perfectly well understood by lawyers like Colas and Gamot. Intensified, recently, by the breakdown of law and order in the province, these grievances were of long standing and of great complexity. The main issue was the tax burden, which had increased continually since the beginning of the century. The expenses of war pushed the government deeper into debt every year. Always short of funds, the Treasury made appalling concessions to financiers. In the last resort, it was the peasantry that footed the bill, since the nobility and the clergy were exempt. Each village was assessed for a lump sum payment. It was up to the village community to divide the total assessment among its member households.

The tax-exemption of the privileged orders infuriated the peasants. More generally, all those who could not claim the privilege of tax-exemption objected to the special status of the nobility. These objections found expression at the highest level. At the Estates General meeting of 1576, the commoners of Dauphiné registered their complaints in a care-, fully composed petition written by Judge de Bourg of Vienne. De Bourg was no peasant. He belonged to one of the most powerful families in the city. He was a seasoned administrator and he was very well educated. The petition in which he summed up the grievances of the Third Estate was a reasoned indictment of royal policy. He explained that the best land was owned by noblemen and priests who paid no taxes, leaving the entire burden to those least able to bear it. He demanded the adoption of fairer principles of taxation. Quoting Cicero, de Bourg challenged the notion of preferential treatment. On what grounds, he asked, were the First and Second Estates exempted from paying their share?

"It will do no good to say they rule over the Third Estate by long precedent, seeing as how there is no custom, privilege, law or ordinance which is not subject to change and correction when evidence and necessity require, as lawgivers have shown and as Plato says in the fourth book of his Laws. . . ." In a community, argued de Bourg, "each and all must share in the conveniences and inconveniences."

The commoners of Dauphiné had argued, throughout the sixteenth century, that taxes ought to be assessed on the value of lands owned, irrespective of the social status of the owner. There was a note of urgency in all these appeals, because more and more of the land was escaping taxation as newly ennobled bourgeois acquired an ever-greater share of the land. Since tax assessments were fixed sums imposed on the village community as a whole, every parcel of land newly declared tax-exempt added to the burden borne by the remaining taxpayers.

Land was changing hands at an alarming rate. About one third of the real estate in the province was sold to new owners in the course of a single generation. Even though taxpaying commoners were still holding on to a respectable 60 percent of the farmland, they were on the defensive, especially in villages easily reached from cities such as Romans, Valence, Montélimar, Vienne, and Grenoble.

The outsiders who bought up rural real estate belonged to the classic *rentier* type, of which Judge Guérin of Romans was a fine example. Well-entrenched within the governing elite of the province, controlling city councils and courts of law, men like Guérin bought land, lent money, and worked at transforming their social status so as to bring tax exemption to their newly purchased domains. Newly ennobled—or merely claiming nobility—they scooped up farmland and removed it from the tax rolls. The number of such "nobles" kept increasing. In the region of Valence alone, for example, the increase of "noblemen" has been estimated at more than 50 percent between 1523 and 1594. The proportion of land removed from the tax rolls reached alarming heights. While taxable property decreased, taxes kept rising and debts mounted. In the village of Bellegarde, for instance, fourteen "nobles" owned two thirds of the land, while the community's debts reached the astronomical figure of 10,000 *écus.*

The victims of these trends, in the first instance, were not landless laborers, but property-owning peasants, whose tax assessments increased in direct proportion to the amount of land that was acquired by tax-exempt outsiders. It is not surprising, then, to find that the agitation against the privileged orders—and, particularly, against the extension of privileges to new nobles—was led by substantial peasants. Village communities hired lawyers to represent their interests. They appealed to the provincial supreme court in Grenoble—and even to the king himself. Occasionally, in the course of this long-standing dispute, concessions were made. In an edict issued in 1548, the king appeared to see the justice of the commoners' cause, since he ruled that all rural property bought by bourgeois since 1518 must be subjected to taxation. This ruling remained a dead letter, because powerful bourgeois like Guérin evaded its provisions by claiming they were not bourgeois. As one of the lawyers representing the Third Estate was to put it, "in fact, the rich are the ones who become nobles."

By the spring of 1578, when village communities were forming leagues and winning their first battles, it seemed that all legal remedies had been exhausted. Neither Grenoble nor Paris seemed willing to reform the tax structure. Village communities were not alone in resenting the privileges of the new nobles. The very same families which claimed tax-exemption in the countryside were also increasing their control over urban politics, provoking the anger of their fellow citizens. Urban leagues, such as the one led by Colas in Montélimar, were putting pressure on the élite ensconced in municipal office. Demands were made for independent audits of municipal budgets. A popular leader like Colas could count on the support of both urban and rural militias when he asked for the ouster of the garrison and for broader participation in city government. There was talk of refusing to pay taxes until inequities were removed.

In February 1579, while Colas, the Prince of Youth from Montélimar, was leading 1,200 armed men against a bandit stronghold, another local hero, Jean Serve, took over the city of Romans without firing a shot. Serve, a man of peasant origin, was, by all accounts, the most popular man in Romans. A master draper by trade, he was well known as a champion player of the popular sport of *paume*, a tennis-like ball game. Serve's nickname was Paumier—the *paume* player. On February 3, on the occasion of the annual feast of St. Blaise, patron saint of the drapers, an armed parade was staged by the members of this trade. It was customary to elect a captain for the drapers' militia on parade. Paumier was elected to this ceremonial post, but this time "they elected a chief, not so much for the occasion, they said, but for the purpose of embracing a cause which they called the rest and relief of the people."

As soon as he had been elected, Paumier took measures to wrest control of the city away from Judge Guérin's political machine. He started packing council meetings with his supporters. He confiscated the keys to the city's gates, making it clear that he would call on the village leagues to join his men in any confrontation to come. Backed by demonstrations in the streets, Paumier demanded "that the balance of accounts be gone over, pertaining to the handling of the communal funds from the year 1564 up to the present; and that the accounts be gone over by those who will be named by the public, so that the oppression caused to the poor people may be stopped."

Paumier's power extended far beyond the walls of Romans. He was allied with the urban league of Valence and he controlled the village leagues of the surrounding area. Paumier's archenemy, Guérin, claimed that the draper's captain could put 14,000 armed men in the field. The village leagues were arming and they chose captains much as Paumier had been chosen in Romans. Assembling to the sound of village church bells, the peasant militia attacked a company of light cavalry so effectively that the soldiers, "after having lost certain men and horses, were forced to take flight," retreating toward Lyon and abandoning horses and weapons. By April, much of the province appeared to be in rebel hands. It was becoming clear that no taxes would be collected in Dauphiné, unless concessions were made.

Responding to the gravity of the situation, the governor sent an agent to Romans to placate Paumier's party and to listen to their grievances. The governor's representative agreed "to force the treasurers and those who have handled municipal funds to give an account of them." Judge Guérin did not believe in concessions. In his view, it was not possible to stop a rebellion, just as it was impossible "to prevent a waterfall from felling all the barriers erected in its path."

Under Paumier's leadership, the leagues assembled in Romans on March 1, 1579, and sent a strike force against the bandit Laprade, at Châteaudouble. Unable to control the leagues, the city council of Romans decided to approve the expedition against Laprade. At the last moment, even the governor, in Grenoble, rode out to join Paumier's improvised army in the assault on Châteaudouble. As soon as the governor had left Grenoble with his bodyguards, the citizens closed the gates behind him and made it clear that they would not allow the soldiers to return. They declared that "the town of Grenoble is of the Union with Vienne, Valence, Romans and others, to free themselves of garrisons and to live in peace." They "wished to guard their towns themselves . . . as good patriots" and to pursue "their just remonstrances," as contained in the petitions presented to the king.

Victorious at Châteaudouble, the leagues pressed their demands: no more soldiers and no more tax-exemptions. At last, the peasant militias began to threaten the nobility, those "who had houses a bit too fine," according to Guérin's account. Now, noted Guérin, the time had come when "the meanest lout thought himself as great a lord as his own *seigneur*." In April, a violent confrontation occurred. A gentleman named Dorbain was rumored to be "gathering noble gentlemen at his house, including certain new nobles"—and it was said "that they were planning to carry out some vengeance." The leagues assembled to march against Dorbain. "Warned of their coming, Dorbain quickly removed himself" from his estate. The peasant militia, "seeing that he was not there, went back to their own place."

The same night Dorbain returned to his house with his armed retainers. He "sent for three of his neighbors, poor laborers who customarily worked for him," questioned them and had them beaten—"leaving them for dead." One of Dorbain's victims, mortally wounded, "revealed everything that had happened." Alerted, "the people gathered to take revenge." Eight hundred or nine hundred strong, the peasants went back to Dorbain's house. Again, Dorbain got away, but this time his house was looted and burned down. On April 19, according to Guérin, Dorbain was killed, at last, "when he went to survey his ruined house." On the same day, the meeting of the provincial Estates opened in Grenoble. The deputies for the Third Estate, led by Judge de Bourg, once again asked for an end to tax-exemptions, while deploring the violence committed by the peasant leagues. The nobility and the clergy remained unmoved; they continued to oppose "the payment of any taxes for property newly acquired from the commons."

From this point on, the alliance between the peasant leagues and the bourgeois grew uneasy. United in their desire to oust the soldiers, to clean up bandit lairs, and to resist unfair taxation, they were divided on the issue of violence. When peasants began to burn castles, their urban allies grew frightened. In Romans, Paumier's leadership was challenged by his close friend, Laroche, who feared reprisals. "If the mutineers continue to do such violence," said Laroche, according to Guérin, "so many will be hanged that the streets will stink from it."

In July, when the queen mother stopped in Montélimar, she spoke with Jacques Colas and came away with the impression that the popular leader was "a presumptuous soul." She would have none of the leagues' demands for tax reform.

"Commoners, pay your taxes," she said. "Do not try to subject the nobility to taxation. Cease to expel my royal garrisons from your towns. Behave peacefully, one and all."

As the queen and her entourage approached Romans, Paumier's men, who held the gates, thought of refusing her entry. At the last minute, they changed their minds.

"Those of the town of Romans," wrote the queen on July 18, "appeared before me in good number. Their captain, known as Paumier, a merchant draper, made me a short address of welcome."

Fully aware of Paumier's power, the queen noted that he had "such great influence and authority over these Leagues that his least word will set those of this town and the surrounding region on the march . . . I would greatly like to speak with him."

When the queen met with Paumier, she asked him: "Why are you against the authority of the King?"

"I am the King's servant," replied Paumier. "But the people have elected me to save the poor folk afflicted by the tyranny of war—and to pursue humbly the just remonstrances contained in their petition."

According to Guérin, Paumier refused to kneel before the queen, "notwithstanding that all the gentlemen present cried loudly to him, several times: 'On your knees!' "

The queen persuaded Paumier to give up the keys to the city's gates. After her departure, the tension between Paumier's party and Guérin's supporters in city hall became unbearable. The armed peasants in the countryside were refusing to pay taxes. Now the butchers and bakers of Romans decided to strike. Winter came. Delegates from the peasant leagues were sent to Grenoble to demand tax reform. No taxes would be paid, said the peasants, until their petition for reform was granted: when the privileged orders paid their share, the peasants would pay their part. The delegates were arrested in Grenoble, where "the people soon whispered of rising up." In January 1580, rumors were rife. The notary Piémont, who kept a diary of the events, noted that "we heard . . . that the nobility was readying several regiments . . . to exterminate the Third

Estate." Judge Guérin was becoming frantic. On February 3, the bishop of Valence could see the peasant militias on the move. From the top of the city's ramparts he watched "a troop of arquebusers who must have numbered five hundred marching in order to the beat of the drum." That evening, the peasants burned a castle to the ground.

In this atmosphere of fear and mutual distrust, Judge Guérin decided to act before it was too late. Fearing that Paumier's supporters in the villages would join him in bringing down the city government, Guérin persuaded Paumier's rival Laroche that the time had come to put an end to the rebellion.

Meanwhile, preparations for the Carnival celebration went ahead. The drapers of Romans "began to march with drums and arms through the town." Paumier, in the lead, was "wearing a robe of bear skin." On February 3, the day of St. Blaise's feast, the streets were filled with six hundred armed men of Paumier's party. According to Guérin, this made the hearts of Paumier and his followers "so greatly swell with pride that he was then assured of being able to carry out his plan, set for the near future."

There was dancing in the streets. Next to the armed drapers, one could make out the members of the Holy Spirit brotherhood, recruited mostly from the poorer, semirural wards of the city. They were dressed in shrouds and carried flails. Some were shouting "that before these days were out, the flesh of Christians would be on sale for six pence a pound." Throughout the wild merrymaking of the Carnival, between St. Blaise's Day and Mardi Gras, the people were heard proclaiming "that the rich of their town had grown rich at the expense of the poor people." The rich were angered, noted Piémont in his diary, as they feared "that restitution would have to be made."

The confrontation was becoming unavoidable. On the evening of February 15, when the richest citizens participated in a masked ball at the city hall, a large crowd of onlookers, including many of Paumier's supporters, stood by to watch the festivities. Suddenly, the masked revelers of Guérin's party charged the crowd, killing and wounding Paumier's men. At the same time, a group of armed men led by Laroche set out for Paumier's house and murdered him. Within the next few hours, Guérin and Laroche managed to rout Paumier's party, which was demoralized and taken by surprise. Securing the city gates, Guérin's men slammed them shut against peasants who were beginning to converge on the city. By morning, Guérin was receiving reinforcements. Hundreds of armed gentlemen responded to his call for help, hunting down peasants in the surrounding villages "like swine." Within two weeks, a special tribunal had been set up to deal with the surviving rebels. The final battle took place on March 26, when the governor led 3,500 soldiers against a peasant militia force. Nine hundred peasants were killed in battle that day and two hundred were taken prisoner, most of them to be killed in cold blood later. Soon the mercenary regiments were back in the province, "overrunning the villages, even up to the gates of Lyon and Vienne, murdering and pillaging all the villages and any towns that were not walled. It was a settling up of their hatred for the league . . . to pillage a poor villager who had no defense but to raise his hands to Heaven," wrote Piémont, in a fitting epitaph for the Dauphiné rebellion.

The defeat of the leagues followed a familiar pattern. While the rebels had the upper hand, the authorities appeared conciliatory, courting rebel leaders with promises; when reinforcements arrived, at last, the local gentry joined in the general massacre. Almost always triggered by new taxes and directed against "outsiders," popular rebellions, seen from the perspective of threatened officials, appeared as tidal waves of unnatural, monstrous dimensions. They could only be explained, in such a perspective, by the secret activities and the personal ambition of the ringleaders. "That unfortunate and damnable conspiracy," in Dauphiné, was not, claimed Judge Guérin, "the invention of a thousand persons," but the treasonable work of a few "ambitious men who wished to increase their wealth and power." Unwilling to entertain the frightening possibility that many of the king's subjects—a majority perhaps—might be truly and deeply disaffected, officials kept insisting that the rebels were only a handful of marginal characters, "persons of little worth," "the lowest part of the people"—"who had nothing to lose."

Historians have tended to accept this point of view. Iniquitous taxes, rapacious lords, and poor harvests, after all, were real enough. It is plausible to imagine that it was the poorest, the most wretched who rebelled. How could one expect discipline, organization, and a program of reforms from such people? Looking at the past from the vantage point of modern revolutions, historians seem secure in their knowledge of what early peasant wars ought to have accomplished. Had they understood their own interests correctly, seventeenth-century peasants would have hurled themselves at their oppressors—and abolished the feudal régime. From such a perspective, it becomes possible to criticize peasant rebels for lacking a well-defined ideology.

But we now know that the revolt in Dauphiné was not carried out by "the lowest part of the people." In Dauphiné and elsewhere the rebels were more likely to be drapers, butchers, carders—men who owned some property and quite a few of whom could read and write. The men of Paumier's party "prided themselves on the fact that they all belonged to the middle level of craftsmen prosperous enough to own homes." As a matter of fact, when the confrontation came, in Romans, Paumier's party was unable to enlist the support of the poor. In the villages, too, the leadership of the rebellion was composed of substantial citizens. Not day laborers, not *journaliers* or *brassiers*—but *laboureurs*, innkeepers, millers, rural bourgeois were in the lead, men, in sum, who had a stake in the established order rather than poor wretches who had nothing to lose.

The organization of rebellions, if Dauphiné is not to be dismissed as an exceptional case, involved the established institutions of rural society. When the church bells summoned the men, they assembled as a community, just as they did when they set out to march in religious processions. Captains were chosen from among the natural leaders of the community. They were men active in the brotherhoods, they were winners of carnival competitions, Princes of Youth, champion racers and marksmen. They were not apprentices, journeymen, or day laborers, not hotheaded youths or beggars, but mature family men with solid reputations.

The rebels did not give battle in the hope of upsetting the social order. They favored peaceful means of resistance. They presented petitions, they formed alliances, they appealed to the ancient laws of the province—and when they fought, they did so to defend rights threatened by usurpers. It is pointless to ask why rebellions did not develop into full-scale class wars pitting peasants against noblemen and poor against rich. It was not the intention of early modern rebels to abolish existing institutions. On the contrary, they were mobilized in defense of the laws as they understood them, against changes introduced by outsiders like Judge Guérin. In the villages, there was no question of landless *brassiers* revolting against the *laboureur* élite. It was the village community as a whole that was prepared to defend its rights against *rentiers* and tax collectors who threatened an ancient equilibrium. Urban revolts, too, are difficult to fit into a modern perspective of revolution. Describing the well-known revolt of 1651 in the city of Bordeaux, a modern historian sees in the rebels' actions "proof of a certain incompleteness, a certain want of maturity."[9] Such an assessment may not be any closer to the mark than had been the judgments of earlier historians who described the Bordeaux rebels as acknowledging "no authority other than mindless fury" and dismissed them as "a blind and bloodthirsty party . . . whose ultimate aim was to transform Bordeaux into a vast cemetery."[10]

As Professor Westrich has shown, the Bordeaux rebels were the same sort of property-owning shopkeepers and artisans who followed Paumier in Romans. Their aim was to challenge the ruling families in city hall. Bordeaux was a major city and a provincial capital. It was filled with hundreds of venal officials of Guérin's sort. The rebels sought to replace these magistrates with new ones "who will render equitable justice." They formed a Union which was modeled on the Craft associations.[11] Their Union was meant to restore the old commune. In Frankfurt, too, rebellious artisans challenged the exclusive privileges of the *Geschlechter* and sought a return to broader participation in government. In all these challenges to authority, the opposition was mobilized by well-established communal institutions—Craft associations, brotherhoods, or ward militias. While officials professed to see only "mindless fury" in these rebellions, the opposition parties always proclaimed their loyalty to king or emperor—not because of "a certain want of maturity," but because of their genuine attachment to the traditions of their community. The specific character of early modern rebellions is to be found in this attachment. It was only in modern times that landless peasants and urban wage-earners would man barricades in the name of abstract revolutionary ideals: they had nothing else to appeal to.

VIII

ON THE MARGINS
OF THE COMMUNITY

In early modern Europe, social conflict tended to remain in the family, so to speak. When the élite in city hall and new landowners in the countryside seemed to bask in excessive privilege, peasants, artisans, and tradesmen might take up arms to defend their rights. The rebels were always well-integrated members of the community. They owned property, they paid taxes, they belonged to Craft associations, village communities, and brotherhoods. Rebellion was directed at outsiders, at those who were thought to threaten the organized community: new nobles in Dauphiné, foreigners in Frankfurt and Valencia, tax collectors everywhere. Apologists for the governing élite pictured the rebels as "the dregs of the people," in the hope of rallying property owners to their cause—and also, to soothe their consciences when the time came to massacre dissidents. Where records permit a close look at who the rebels were, we do not see derelicts and thieves—but butchers, tanners, brewers, shopkeepers, and lawyers' clerks participating in urban insurrections. The conflict always remained a struggle for power among native citizens, men related to each other, men who had been friends, who knew each other well, who were linked to each other by their business or professional activities, men entitled to vote in municipal elections.

What of the disenfranchised, the disinherited, the poor, the drifters, and beggars who slept in the streets—all those who lived on the margins of the community? They could be found milling about in the general confusion, like extras on a movie set, but their participation in rebellions remained as marginal as was their participation in the community's affairs in times of peace. Paying no taxes, having no voice in village or town meetings, left out of the brotherhoods and Craft associations, these were the people on the bottom of the heap, capable of theft, murder, arson, and individual acts of desperation, but impotent as a group.

Yet their numbers were large. Cities were crowded with thousands of unemployed men and women driven away from their native villages by hunger. Alien paupers joined native paupers who had been rendered helpless by depressed wages, rising food prices, and personal tragedies such as illness or the death of a husband. The numbers of the poor—of those who would starve unless aided by the community—were formidable. Depending on the definition of poverty we use, we will find, in the sixteenth century, as many as 10 percent of the households in Valladolid—15 percent in Segovia—listed as poor and exempted from tax payments for this reason. In the eighteenth century, a figure of 20 percent in a middling town such as Bayeux is in no sense exceptional.[1]

To the native poor, who show up in census figures, because they have a permanent residence, we must add immigrants looking for work, vagrants, and beggars. Municipal authorities distinguished between native and foreign paupers, singling their own hard-pressed citizens out for charity and driving foreigners out whenever possible, after a modest handout for the road. In times of famine and plague it became especially important to control this permanent underclass of men, women, and children who begged in the streets and slept huddled together in slums from which infectious disease was likely to spread to the homes of the propertied classes.

At such times, the town crier would be sent through the streets, to announce that all beggars must assemble in the central square on Sunday afternoon to be counted, on pain of expulsion from the city.[2] Native paupers without shelter could be locked up in hospices; foreign ones could be sent on their way. Half-starved, exhibiting their sores to prompt charity, this floating population had little hope of being rescued. Poorhouses, hospices, alms distributed in churches and in city halls—all these institutionalized attempts to relieve poverty were of little consequence, given the numbers of those in need. According to one historian's estimate, the resources available for official poor relief in most of eighteenth-century France could not have stretched to provide more than a single pound of bread annually for each hungry person.[3]

Beggars were the most visible and openly distressing category of people living on the margins of the community. Unable to pay taxes, landless, without property and without employment, such people had slipped through the network of solidarities available to the working population. It did not take much to push farmhands or weavers from their precarious position in the community. Poor to begin with, they became destitute at the slightest shift within the wage and price structure. An able-bodied man who owned nothing could live on his wages. But once he married and fathered children he was on his way to helplessness. More than one third of adult Frenchmen earned less than 17 *sols* daily, at a time when it took 35 *sols* to buy enough bread to feed a couple and three young children.[4] As for women, who earned less than men, if their husbands became incapacitated, if their husbands died—or took to the road, one day, overwhelmed by their losing struggle to provide—then there was no way they could make ends meet. The widow of a minor artisan was condemned to a life of poverty. No matter how promising things might have looked on her wedding day, such a woman would end her life in need of charity. A silkworker, like Jeanne Michon, of the city of Lyon, who had brought a dowry of 300 *livres* to her bridegroom, a master silk weaver, was left, at her husband's death, with nothing but a bed, a sheet, and a worn blanket. Widowed lacemakers, earning less than 6 *sols* a day, were trying to feed their children on this pittance. These are not isolated cases. Of the 310 households receiving public charity in the town of Bayeux, 70 were headed by widows with an average of three children— and a further 52 households were headed by women abandoned by their husbands.

Rural poverty was no different. Landless—or nearly landless—farm laborers took a fatal step toward eventual indigence if they married. The children of such marriages swelled the ranks of the beggar population. A French village with a total population of 808, reported 31 paupers who were too old or infirm to earn their keep—and 77 beggars, most of whom were children. Another village listed 50 beggar children in a population of 930.[5]

All such paupers—widows, old people, children—fell into the broad category of the deserving poor. It was understood that they were helpless through no fault of their own, and some attempt was made to alleviate their misery. Begging children were tolerated. They came around after the harvest, making off with odds and ends. They picked fallen fruit off the ground, they gathered sorrel, acorns, dandelion leaves, dug for clams along the beaches, carried off fishheads at the marketplace.

Abandoned children were cared for by the community. In a city like Valladolid, perhaps as many as 10 percent of the babies born and baptized in a given year were abandoned on the doorsteps of churches, convents, and the houses of the rich.[6] These *niños expositos* were offered shelter in orphanages, but their chances of surviving were not good. Most of the children abandoned by their parents were infants born to unwed mothers. These babies were placed in the local poorhouse or shipped off to cities equipped with foundling hospitals. Child transporters made a living carrying infants for a fee. In the eighteenth century, one might meet them on French highways, heading for Paris. The child transporter, according to one observer, "is a man who carries on his back newborn infants, in a padded box that can hold three of them. They are upright in their swaddling clothes, breathing the air from the top. The man stops only to eat and drink and to let them suck a little milk [by means of a sponge]. When he opens his box, he often finds one dead. He finishes his journey with the two others, impatient to be rid of his load. When he has left them at the hospital, he starts back at once, in order to resume the same job by which he earns his daily bread." Most of the babies shipped off in this way never made it to their destination.[7]

The women who gave up their babies did so because they themselves lived on the margins of their community. They were usually unmarried servant girls of rural origin, for whom the birth of a child was a disaster. Such girls had not the slightest chance of avoiding the beggar's life unless they worked from dawn to dusk, for years on end, in the hope of amassing a dowry which would allow them to return to their village some day and find a husband. Having left home when they were about fourteen, they would spend some ten years in the city, trading their energy and their willingness to work long hours for the prospect of an eventual toehold in their community. They ate scraps and slept under the stairs, putting away their paltry wages. All cities had a large complement of maidservants of this kind. They carried water, they cleaned and swept, they did the laundry, and they hired out to weavers and lacemakers in the evenings. They made up something like 10 percent of the urban population. Their daily struggle to achieve eventual independence was always threatened by the fear of pregnancy. They were, of course, highly vulnerable to seduction by their masters.[8]

A child born to a servant girl was bound to destroy her own chance of ever becoming integrated into the community. Abandoned on the steps of a church, the infant was given at least a small chance. Prosperous cities like Valladolid or Rouen maintained orphanages where children were sheltered and trained according to their capacities. Boys were taught to read and write and apprenticed to various artisans. The Valladolid orphanage, in the course of a single year, managed to place 46 boys between the ages of eleven and sixteen with tailors, shoemakers, jewelers, barbers, and other craftsmen. Gifted boys received a Latin education and a number of girls were provided with small dowries, in the hope that they would find a husband.[9] Even the abandoned children of slave girls, once admitted to a foundling hospital, were declared free and absorbed into the work force, in the labor-hungry cities of the fifteenth century.[10]

The number of children rescued in this way was small, to be sure, but the efforts made in their behalf testify to the good intentions of the leading citizens, who understood perfectly well that masses of beggars represented a serious threat to the community. Saving a few children was, perhaps, no more than an ineffectual gesture meant to ward off the proliferation of the destitute. In bad years, when hunger stalked the streets and the rural poor flocked to the cities in desperation, the rich acknowledged that Nature had her own methods for solving the problem: Disease disposed of the poor, "whose death is without importance," observed a merchant in Valladolid.[11]

Assisting the needy was a moral duty, but of the masses of the poor, only a small proportion were deemed worthy of relief. The rest, the "unworthy beggars," were more likely to inspire fear than charity. This fear was well founded, since there never was the slightest hope of rehabilitation for the mass of adult beggars who drifted from town to town in search of employment and handouts.

Living on the margins of the community, the poor had no way of making their weight felt in the political process. They could not influence elected officials to legislate in their favor. Rejected by the stable society of rural and urban householders, they were in no position to provoke rebellions. Helpless against the mighty, they were capable of threatening the vulnerable. Moving along in small bands, they could descend on isolated farms, extorting gifts by threatening to set fire to a barn. The roads were crowded with penniless men and women whose lives fluctuated between seasonal employment, begging, and crime.

Once ejected from their native villages, these people who did not belong anywhere, who acknowledged no masters, were hard to classify. Some were migrant workers who returned to their cottages regularly. Desolate mountain villages exported their laboring poor as a matter of course. Typical of such villages, where expatriation was the only means of livelihood available, is St. Jean d'Ollières, a village in the French Massif Central, where only the women and the younger children stayed home. Out of a total population of 1,190 adults and 810 children, 200 men would leave, every year, in October, to cut wood. They returned, nine months later, to spend two weeks tending to farm chores before heading south for the olive harvest in Provence. Another 200 men and 100 children would leave in November, to comb hemp in the fields of another province. Those among them who could not find work would move on to

Paris, to beg and to do odd jobs. They could not return home before Easter, since there would be no food for them. In the spring, having plowed their fields, they headed south to pick mulberry leaves for the silkworms until the summer was over. Another 300 children from the same village left home every year to work as chimney sweeps. Others still, too young or too old to do heavy work, hit the road to beg. They carried a supply of combs to sell. Or else they relied on well-rehearsed hard-luck stories to engage the sympathy of charitable folk along the way. They were often equipped with letters delivered by their parish priest which testified to their honest misery.[12]

Side-by-side with inoffensive beggars, there were those who turned to crime. The young man who earned an honest living in the summer became an unemployed vagrant in the fall, with no resources for months to come—and no place to go back to. Once he had been ejected from the constraints imposed by his family and by his neighbors, he was on his own. He feared nothing, except the gallows. The policing powers of early modern states were rudimentary. Little progress was made in the direction of controlling dangerous vagrants. Theft, of course, was the most common crime. A boy caught stealing a shirt risked being punished in the most brutal and arbitrary way. He might be branded with a hot iron, the letter V, for vagrant, seared into his flesh. He might be sentenced to the king's galleys—or he might be hanged on the spot.[13] Few offenders were arrested, but when a dangerous drifter was caught, at last, he might confess, under torture, to an astonishing series of crimes.

The confession of young John Brown—Jehan Le Brun—extracted from him in Paris, in 1389, may serve as an example of such hopeless cases. John's father was a soldier, his mother a camp follower. The parents, apparently, fulfilled their duty to John, apprenticing him to a blacksmith. His apprenticeship completed, John left to become a journeyman smith in Rouen, but he was soon diverted from honest employment, finding the soldier's life more to his taste. He served for a time, but soon deserted, stealing a horse and galloping off to Paris, where he sold the horse and lost his money gambling in taverns. He joined the army again, briefly, but soon took up with criminals in whose company he murdered a prostitute and sold her clothes. From then on his life became a steady succession of crimes.[14]

Crime as a profession was the end of a long road traveled by those who had no property. The pressures that turned hired hands into criminals never let up. As an observer put it, in 1763, "the peasant leaves his village and comes to beg in the cities only when he is pushed by the most imperious need. Often, he becomes a beggar without meaning harm—and soon turns into a thief and murderer. The society he frequents corrupts him gradually, until he is led to commit the worse crimes."

There was nothing mysterious about these developments. A commission of inquiry described the problem with perfect candor: "a large city, where many roads converge, constantly attracts an infinite number of idle persons—unruly parasites, or wage earners entirely dependent on the work of their hands. The slighest illness condemns their family to horrible poverty: this is why our streets, our squares, even our churches are filled and covered by beggars."[15]

Dangerous vagrants rarely acted alone. They formed partnerships and proceeded in small groups, seeking work on the farms and showing up at regular bread distributions in monasteries along the way. On the road, they joined up with others who spoke their language, who came from the same province. In the cities, they made straight for slums already occupied by compatriots who would help them find odd jobs—or initiate them into the workings of the underworld.

This propensity for forming associations was a natural response to the isolation that threatened men without family and without community. Far away from their original communities, men on the move tended to create new ones. Beggars were said to be organized in secret companies which elected their own leaders. According to the testimony of a teenage beggar arrested in Rome, in 1595, Roman beggars belonged to fellowships resembling the Craft associations. There were the *grancetti*, who specialized in purse snatching; the *sbasiti*, who pretended to be ill, stretched out in the street and moaning; the "barons," who begged standing up and claimed to be temporarily out of work. The informant went on to name 19 specialized begging companies.[16]

Vagrancy had a way of leading to banditry. Wherever more than four persons were involved in a theft, French law suspected organized crime—and meted out death sentences.[17] Punishment was not calculated to fit the crime, but to act as a deterrent. It was not the amount of damage done that counted in the judges' minds, but the likelihood of criminal actions spreading to ever-larger numbers of potential delinquents. An easy theft—the theft of a loaf of bread from a street stall, for instance—could be punished with stupefying severity. A three-year term of forced labor in the King's ships was close enough to a death sentence, since the chained convicts were not likely to survive the treatment they received.[18]

Even though they were always on the move, outlaws tended to reconstitute a semblance of community. Vagrants, deserters, prostitutes, and orphans were associated in gangs that terrorized the countryside. These gangs benefited from the complicity of the local poor. They had little to fear from ineffective, corrupt, and outnumbered police forces. Their victims preferred to pay protection money rather than risk reprisal in the event of denunciation. The fear of gangs was so well established that clever rogues acting on their own would pretend to represent an organized band in their attempts to extort money. Nicolas Péreau, an unemployed servant, used this stratagem. He composed a threatening letter and delivered it to his intended victims on Christmas Eve. Speaking in the name of "ten poor couples," Péreau wrote: "we wil go to yar farm to get a chantribushon we wants hunnert franks eech . . . be gud enuf to put it to the red gait bye Saint Charl ousid nekst to the Wal at fife oclok be shoor to do it or else . . . we wil set fyre to al yor farm." When Péreau was arrested, he admitted that he had "said we were ten in order to scare people."[19]

Gangs were real enough, though, and they were far more effective threats to property and public order than were thieves working on their own. Sedentary gangs took care never to alienate the local people. They attacked outsiders, merchants or travelers. The proceeds of their robberies found their way to the local markets and fairs. Typical of this kind of gang was the bandit family led by a young Breton woman in the village of Faouët in the 1770s. Marion, the leader of the gang, had started out as a servant girl in the seaport city of Lorient. She lost her job when she was 21. She moved back to the village to live with her mother. Pregnant, now, she took up the family trade of peddler, an occupation barely distinguishable from begging. Marion's mother, Helen Kerneau, who had been married twice, was listed as a beggar in her marriage record. Marion soon went into a more dangerous—and more lucrative—kind of business, in partnership with her brothers, stepbrothers, nephews, sisters, brothers-in-law, and various lovers and friends. For a good ten years, Marion's gang engaged in highway robbery, enjoying the complicity of the neighbors.[20]

Roving gangs could be anything from a small operation enlisting half a dozen orphans and teenage runaways led by an adult deserter—to bands said to number as many as 300 members, capable of moving through an entire province, on foot and on horseback, armed to the teeth and safe from challenges, short of the arrival of a regiment of cavalry.

Banditry, especially when it involved smuggling, could turn murderous deserters into folk heroes. Attacking the rich, preying on tax collectors, and feared by the salt and tobacco monopolies, bandit chieftains achieved fame for their daring exploits. They became Robin Hoods in the popular imagination. Of the Catalan bandit leader Rocaguinarda, whose misdeeds made him famous between 1602 and 1611, a contemporary reported that "he was the most courteous bandit to have been in that region for many years: never did he dishonor or touch churches, and God aided him." Of the Italian bandit Marco Sciarra, who achieved fame in the 1580s, the poor of Naples used to say, hopefully, "that he would soon come to occupy Naples and make himself King." Sciarra virtually controlled the impoverished countryside around Rome, replacing established authority to the point of appointing local judges and performing marriage ceremonies. In the mountain strongholds of southern Spain, the bandits of the Sierra de Cabrilla were famous for dressing elegantly and for their kindness and courtesy to their victims, whom they robbed of only half their goods. They were known as *los beatos de Cabrilla,* the holy ones of Cabrilla. A Castilian bandit named Pedro Andreu was rumored to have 30—or even 80—horsemen. It was believed that "he never kills anyone, but takes only part of their money, leaving them with enough to continue their journey and that he borrows money from villages and individuals, giving his word as pledge and is punctual in payment."[21]

An undue fascination with crime can mislead historians into a false assessment of the floating population feared by the authorities. Beggars and vagrants are known to us primarily from criminal records. The massive population of traveling men did produce arsonists and thieves. But so did the main body of peasants who never left home. Who can establish which group was more given to violence? Peasants resorted to threats of arson when they lost their leases. Poor or well-to-do, peasants were capable of burning down the house they were evicted from. The courts, if they investigated cases of this sort, came up against a wall of silence. The law expressly forbade "all inhabitants, tenants, plowmen and others . . . to molest landowners and new tenants . . . to hinder or discourage, by threats or otherwise, those who might apply for the lease of the said properties," but peasants held to their own unshakable belief in the rights they had established. They refused to accept the notion that leases held by their parents and grandparents before them, could be revoked under any circumstances. And they burned down barns to make their point. The potential for violence existed both within settled communities and in the nebulously defined world of migrants.[22]

And yet it was the world of the traveling men that attracted the notice of the authorities, in whose eyes men without families constituted an automatic threat to law and order. In the case of beggars and unemployed vagrants, these fears may have been justified. But in the case of traveling journeymen—another large category of men without families—the suspicions of the courts appear misplaced.

Judging from the fragmentary evidence available to us, traveling journeymen were not organized for criminal purposes. Their calling was an ancient and honorable one, which survived into the twentieth century. Journeymen were, nevertheless, always under suspicion. Beginning in the sixteenth century, they were forced to go underground. Official distrust of journeymen proceeded from several motives. There was, first of all, the assumption that young men away from home were bound to cause trouble. Away from the authority of his parents and the watchful eyes of his neighbors, how could a traveling shoemaker or mason be expected to remain law-abiding, unless he was placed under the firm rule of his employer?

The good behavior of journeymen, in earlier times, had been linked to their own expectations of achieving a master's status, of marrying and establishing their own households. Relations between masters and journeymen had once resembled the workings of a family. In the course of the sixteenth century, these relations changed. From then on, many journeymen could no longer have realistic expectations of eventual independence. Lacking capital, they were becoming permanent wage earners, hired out to a succession of masters who paid the lowest possible wages and who let them go when orders slackened. It was no longer the family, but the market economy that began dictating conditions in the workplace. Journeymen carpenters, roof layers, or printers were turning into an urban proletariat. Their livelihood became as precarious—and as subject to the whims of employers—as was that of hired hands in the rural economy.

Journeymen began to organize to defend their interests—and that was what the authorities objected to. Spurred on by the complaints of masters who were outraged by the independent ways of journeymen, magistrates declared journeymen's associations illegal. The result, predictably, was that the journeymen were driven into ever closer and more secret forms of cooperation.

The world of the traveling journeyman, known to us from occasional police reports and from diaries and reminiscences, was a formal world, full of rules and ceremonies, a mirror image, in fact, of the formal associations, guilds, fellowships, and youth clubs the journeymen had known before they took up the wandering life. The original purpose of taking to the road had been to learn the secrets of the craft from a variety of masters. This remained the acknowledged purpose of these long journeys, which could take a man along fixed itineraries, stretching to hundreds of miles, and might take years to complete. But it was no longer expected that the journeyman, his *Wanderjahre* or his *Tour de France* behind him, would return home to found a family. It was more likely that he would spend a good part of his life on the road. Having no property other than his tools, which he carried in a satchel, together with a few clothes and a crust of bread, the traveling journeyman could easily be mistaken for just another vagrant. Such a confusion he wished to avoid at all costs.

Skilled workingmen went to great lengths to establish their special status on the road. They traveled in small groups of three or four men belonging to the same trade. They exhibited special marks, known only to the initiated, of membership in their brotherhood. A sturdy wooden staff cut to a precise length, with a ribbon of a significant color tied to it, might be sufficient to recognize a colleague. A hat, worn in a particular way, was another signal. A secret handshake was a further proof of membership. In his satchel, the journeyman carried papers which were to be hidden from the authorities. On arrival in a strange city, traveling journeymen knew which tavern they should go to: here they got in touch with the local cell of the brotherhood. They were met by the *mother*, often a woman innkeeper, who acted as the local caretaker. They displayed their walking papers, and if everything was in order, the *mother* would arrange for room and board, while the local placement agent would find a job for them.

The journeymen's brotherhoods prevented employers from hiring and firing men arbitrarily. Backed up by their organization, journeymen were not completely at the mercy of their masters. The contractor who dared to hire carpenters who were not members of their union, faced the threat of strikes. Scabs feared for their lives and uncooperative employers could be blackballed: traveling journeymen could be warned off from stopping in a town altogether. On the other hand, the employer who cooperated with the journeymen's associations received certain guarantees. The men he hired were honor-bound to do good work. They would not skip out before the job was completed, and they would not steal. The union vouched for them. Offenders ran the risk of expulsion. No man could leave town without having his papers signed by the local agent, who certified that he had done honest work and paid his dues. A member in good standing, having completed his assignment, would be sent on his way with all the marks of honor he was entitled to, including a formal send-off.[23]

The traveling journeyman was not a member of a community in the ordinary sense, but he had joined a community of his own making which protected him in times of need and from which he derived his reputation and identity. He earned a professional nickname. He was proud of his trade and intent on living up to the reputation he had established, even if outsiders eyed him with suspicion. Deprived of the advantages of citizenship, he had the satisfaction of despising those who were not members of his secret fellowship. He was a free man, and, as such, he was envied by those who were disenfranchised without enjoying the compensating benefits of membership in a fellowship of their own.

Beggars and bandits, at times, also created countercultures of their own, speaking secret jargons, electing leaders and improvising formal rituals to replace those reserved for respectable bourgeois. There was one category of persons, however, among those excluded from membership in officially acknowledged communities, for which no such claims can be made: slaves.

Slaves were a truly marginal group. In most of Western Europe they were not to be found at all. But there were exceptions. Along the Mediterranean shores, where merchants maintained business relationships with Muslim traders, slavery was practiced openly. If the practice rarely affected most European cities and villages, it was not because of moral scruples—but, simply, because there was only a very limited demand for slave labor in Europe. When the African slave trade became profitable, with the opening of sugar cane plantations in the Atlantic islands—and, eventually, in the Caribbean, and on the American mainland—Christian traders did not hesitate to traffic in human beings. The Atlantic slave trade created some spin-off effects in Spain and Portugal. There were thousands of slaves in Lisbon, for a time the silver mines of southern Spain employed African slaves, a monastery in Seville listed 6,327 slaves among its assets, in 1565, and hundreds of slaves could be found working in the busy port of Cadiz. The presence of slaves in the Iberian peninsula may serve as a reminder of the frontier character of the southern borderlands, recently reconquered from Muslim princes.

Even in Lisbon, Seville, or Cadiz, slaves were common only during the boom years of the sixteenth century.[24] Elsewhere, European society can be described as the only slave-proof region in the world. It had no more use for slaves in its work force in 1600 than in 1900. Exceptional circumstances alone could create a market for slaves in Western Europe. Aside from the halcyon days of the Atlantic slave trade, when African slaves could be bought cheaply in Spanish and Portuguese seaports, there was only one clearly circumscribed moment when slaves could be found in large numbers in some European cities. It is worth taking a close look at this event because of what it can tell us about Western attitudes toward slavery.

The moment in question is the century or so following the first ravages of the Black Death which resulted in an unprecedented labor shortage, especially in the great cities of the Mediterranean zone. Although slavery had certainly existed before the year 1000, it had gradually disappeared in the course of the great population expansion of the eleventh and twelfth centuries. The dislocation of the labor market, after 1347, moved Italian and Spanish merchants to start importing slaves from the Muslim East.

There may have been some initial show of reluctance toward this forgotten and disreputable trade. A Florentine decree of 1363, for instance, permitted the importation of slaves—but, on condition that they were infidels, not Christians. The restriction was probably not very significant, since slaves bought in Muslim markets were not likely to be Christian in the first place—and if, by chance, an Armenian Christian was included in a shipment to Italy, who would know the difference? The Church, in Italy and in Spain, did not take a clear stand on the issue of slavery. In practice, bishops tended to approve, popes accepted presents of slaves, and priests were content to own them. Insisting, on the one hand, that only infidel slaves may be imported, the Church demanded, on the other hand, that slaves, once they had landed in Christian territory, be baptized and give Christian names. On the question of the treatment of slaves, once they had become the property of Christians, the Church was silent.

The merchants who brought slaves to the Italian markets were not especially tenderhearted creatures. There is no reason to think that they treated their cargo with a solicitude any more remarkable than that habitually displayed by the Arab slavers whose lessons they had absorbed. Slaves were sold to brokers in the ports, for eventual resale. The bills of sale show that the newly purchased slave was merely property, "to have, hold, sell, exchange, enjoy, rent, dispose of in his will, to judge, soul and body, and to do with whatever may please him, in accordance with his own pleasure."[25]

Slaves were relatively inexpensive in the fourteenth and early fifteenth centuries, when the Genoese imported them in large numbers. On the

Venetian market alone, it seems that something like 10,000 slaves were sold, between 1414 and 1423. A merchant who paid 30 florins for a good horse, and 68 florins for a damask wedding gown, could buy a ten-year-old slave girl for 50 florins, as high a price as could be commanded, because girls nearing puberty were particularly expensive. Another indication of the worth of a slave can be gleaned from an inventory of a farmer's assets, which notes, dryly, that "he says that he has a female slave and a horse and two donkeys and three fifths of an ox. Let us put them down at 70 florins." A Genoese merchant, finding that his slave girl was pregnant, did not hesitate to order the liquidation of his damaged goods: "you may throw her in the sea, with what she has in her belly," he wrote to his agent, "for it is no creature of mine."[26]

In spite of plentiful supplies, reasonable prices, and no special reservations concerning the morality of the slave trade, it did not establish itself in Europe. Although it flourished, briefly, in the Mediterranean ports, it soon dried up, not because of prohibitions, but because there was no permanent place for slaves in the European economy. Only an exceptional region like Sicily, where large estates were the rule and where independent peasant communities never existed, was open to slave labor. Elsewhere, there simply was no place for slaves in the work force, except as domestic servants.

This was the market the slave traders concentrated on. Their stock in trade consisted of young girls from the Black Sea region—captured Tartars, Circassians, Armenians, Russians. Judging from the proportion of female as opposed to male slaves reaching Italian harbors—and keeping in mind the prices fetched by girls—this was a specialized trade. Twelve-year-old Tartar girls, bought in Tana, at the mouth of the Don River, were particularly prized. There is little doubt that sexual exploitation was the chief lure, even though the poor creatures were not likely to reach their destination without blemishes and scars. They were handled roughly in transit. Stowed in the hold of the ship, they were cut and marked on their faces and hands and, more likely than not, raped by sailors during the sea voyage.

A slave girl's place within her owner's family was that of a servant—but of a servant who could be abused with impunity. Slaves received no wages and they could not quit if they were mistreated. In the late fourteenth century, when the free work force was decimated by disease, wages were high, so that the purchase of a slave could be viewed as a rational investment. The price of a slave girl was about the same as that of a mule, equivalent, roughly, to eight years' wages for a free servant. A teenage girl bought at the Venetian slave auctions was an investment that would start paying off in a few years' time. Meanwhile the girl could be taken advantage of. The hardest tasks in the household were for her.

"Pray buy me a little slave girl, young and sturdy," wrote the merchant Datini to his agent in Genoa. "I want her only to wash the dishes and to carry the wood and the bread to the oven." But wives knew better. When Datini sent a slave girl to his friend Paparo, who had asked him to pick one up in Genoa or Venice, there was trouble right away. When the girl arrived in Paparo's household, she turned out to be young and pretty. Datini never heard the end of it. "Paparo's wife complains greatly of you," he was soon advised. Signora Paparo was upset that Signora Datini "should allow you to send such a young and fair slave. She says she never would do such a thing to her, and women should take heed not to do such things to each other." The women's fears were entirely justified. Unwanted pregnancies among slave girls were so frequent that the Foundling Hospital in Florence was to shelter more than one thousand babies abandoned by slave mothers between 1395 and 1485. In the city of Lucca, one third of the abandoned infants had slave mothers.[27]

In spite of the evident advantages of using slave girls as domestic servants, the practice did not take hold. The European family was different from the Oriental family. Italian wives had the power to resist the intrusion of this foreign element into their households. And the men knew it. A Venetian merchant who had just bought an eighteen-year-old slave girl for a friend of his, advised him: "If you wish to keep her for yourself, I'm afraid Lisa [his friend's wife] will think her too pretty." Even Datini, who lived separated from his wife Margherita, could not bring himself to treat slave girls as chattel, to be used and disposed of at will. He bought slaves, but he treated them much as he treated his free servants. When he seduced a free maid servant, Datini took care of her. Twelve-year-old Ghirigora, for instance, whom he hired in 1383, soon shared Datini's bed. When she became pregnant, he arranged to have her marry a poor farmer, providing a large sum of money and two chests filled with clothes and household goods as a dowry. With a slave girl who bore him a child, Datini acted even more responsibly. The baby was "secretly placed in the hospital of S. Maria Nuova" and, later, raised by foster parents at Datini's expense, because Signora Datini wanted to have nothing to do with the slave girl's child. However, when little Ginevra was six years old, the Datinis reached a reasonable compromise. Datini arranged for Ginevra's mother, the slave Lucia, to marry a servant. In exchange, having thus gotten rid of her rival, Signora Datini agreed, at last, to take in little

Ginevra, to raise her as her own. Ginevra was taught to read and showered with affection. At fifteen, Ginevra, the daughter of a slave, was engaged to be married to the cousin of a friend of the Datinis. Her dowry and her wedding cost Datini a very handsome sum of money.[28]

Not all slaves, to be sure, could have been as lucky. But there is no reason to think that the Datini household was exceptional in its attitude toward slaves. Slaves could inspire fear. "They are bestial women," complained Signora Datini. "You cannot trust the house to such as they. They might, at any time, rise up against you."[29] As long as they were perceived as alien, slaves were feared. But it did not take long for slaves to become members of the family, even without the intimacy of the bedroom. Italy was not, after all, a slave society. All but the domestic sphere was closed to slave labor. Within the household, within the neighborhood, slaves were heavily outnumbered. They adapted, they took on the ways of other servants, they moved easily into freedom. Datini reports the following incident involving the well-named Argomento, a male slave whom he had freed and who continued to work for him. Argomento, when reprimanded for failing to look after a mule properly, "took his leave and said he would rather eat grass than be spoken to like that."[30]

Unlike the plantation economies of the New World, where slaves outnumbered their masters and were consequently feared and treated as dangerous prisoners, the households of fourteenth-century Italy absorbed slaves and assimilated them. Slave girls ended up as wives and their children were integrated into the community, for even foundlings of slave origin were declared free, given shelter, and apprenticed, eventually, within the city. Slaves who adapted poorly—and those who were unfortunate in their masters—might end up committing crimes for which they were punished with exemplary brutality. As the Mediterranean slave trade dried up, in the sixteenth century, slavery was viewed, increasingly, as an aberration peculiar to the Americas. Even though French or English capital was invested in the overseas slave trade, the peculiar institution was not countenanced on European territory. When a trader tried to offer slaves for sale in the French port of Bordeaux, in 1571, the local courts refused permission, on the ground that "France, the Mother of Liberty, does not allow slaves." A French jurist, in 1608, summed matters up in this way: "All persons are free in this kingdom and, as soon as a slave reaches our border, and is baptized, he must be considered free."[31]

IX

PRIVATE LIVES

If slavery could not find a permanent home in Western Europe, this was due, in part, to the strength of the family. In this society where tribal or caste forms of organization were absent, the family was unchallenged as the most fundamental and the most powerful link between individuals. There was no place in this society for single persons without property. Slave girls and their progeny, if they survived, were absorbed by households like that of the Datinis. Less fortunate slaves, those forced to work in the dreaded silver mines, for instance, were not likely to live long. The same was true, no doubt, of slaves employed as rowers in Mediterranean ships. One cannot help wondering about the eventual fate of the little mulatto boy purchased by a Spanish village priest in 1570. Although he was guaranteed to be "neither a thief, nor given to fleeing or drunkenness, in good health and clean," there could be no future for the boy in the village, unless he remained a lifelong dependent of the priest's household.[1]

Even native villagers reduced to single status by misfortune were in danger of being rejected by the community, as if they were foreign bodies. Lacking a family and lacking an inheritance, such persons could expect harassment. A teenaged and destitute orphan could find little sympathy, unless he hired on as a servant, joining a household and thus becoming a member of a family. Living alone was bound to lead to trouble, as in the case of young Jusepe Rodriguez who was denounced by several householders in a village near Toledo, in southern Spain, in December 1609. The boy had been seen loitering near some chicken coops. He was arrested, taken to Toledo, and brought before the magistrate on suspicion of theft. The judge ordered the boy to find work. Failing that, he would be banished from his native village.

Single women ran the risk of being accused of "scandalous and dishonest behavior." A married woman whose husband was away, serving in the galleys or in the army, could be charged with "running around and doing many scandalous things." The judge would then declare that she should "go and find her husband and live with him again." Young women whose parents had died and who lacked sufficient property to find a husband were seen as a threat to the community. Automatically suspected of immoral behavior, such women would be denounced, sooner or later, and magistrates would be asked to banish them.[2]

Left stranded by the death of their parents or by the disappearance of a husband, dishonored by the birth of an illegitimate child—or, simply, unable to find a marriage partner for want of an inheritance—single persons found themselves accused of sexual misconduct, theft, or even witchcraft. Woe to the younger son who had no inheritance, to the daughter who refused to marry the only available party. The secret torments experienced by girls pushed into marriage against their inclination rarely stand recorded in official documents, even though their plight was clearly one of the most common dilemmas of the time and the subject of innumerable popular plays, stories, and songs. On occasion, even judicial archives preserve such private tragedies.

Take the lawsuit brought by François Martin, in January 1529, against young Catherine Gent, for breach of promise. Catherine's father was dead and her mother was determined to assure her daughter's future by marrying her off to Martin. Preliminary agreement for the eventual marriage had been reached by the two families. Catherine had accepted a gift from her intended. She had allowed herself to be engaged to Martin in a public ceremony, in front of the parish church. All that was lacking now was her consent to proceed with the wedding. This she refused to give.

In court, Catherine was represented by a lawyer who took the position that the girl's promises had been obtained by means of threats. She had been taken to the church against her will. And even admitting that she had promised to marry Martin, she could not be expected to proceed with the marriage since the bridegroom was known to be impotent.

Testifying in Catherine's favor, her sixteen-year-old girl friend Edmonne confirmed that Catherine never wanted to marry Martin. Whenever her mother urged the marriage on her, Catherine would say, in the witness's hearing: "Mother, dear Mother, please do not make me marry him. . . . If you are tired of taking care of me, let me go and be a servant." The witness Edmonne added that the accused was always crying and that she had seen her on her knees, begging for her married older sister's help: "My dear sister," she would cry, "please tell Mother she must not do this to me. If she does, I will be the most unhappy person in the family."

Asked whether the accused was crying on her way to church, on the evening of the engagement, Edmonne replied that she did not know, because it was too dark to see. Asked whether Catherine was engaged to Martin of her own accord, Edmonne said that, in her opinion, Catherine was engaged against her will, because she could be seen resisting and backing away, until someone grabbed her arm and led her toward the priest, saying: "Here she is." Furthermore, just before the engagement, Catherine's mother had threatened the girl in front of the witness, saying: "You dirty bedbug, by God, if you do not take him you will not have a penny from me and I will treat you so badly that everyone will feel sorry for you. You ugly bedbug! Find a master and go away, for I shall not let you stay with me if you do not marry him!"

"Very well, Mother," Catherine was heard to reply. "I will be content to become a serving maid. If you do not want me to go into service, I would have you kill me rather than marrying him—and I will forgive you my death."[3]

Catherine's experience naturally engages our sympathy, since, in our view, a woman's free choice of a husband ought to be her undoubted right. The remarkable thing is that such a right was largely conceded in the sixteenth century. The reason why Catherine Gent was subjected to so much pressure is that the girl really did have the power to refuse the marriage. Disobeying her mother surely entailed serious consequences, but if she felt strongly enough about it, Catherine could put a stop to the entire proceeding because marriage was a contract—and no contract was valid unless freely entered into by both contracting parties. That is why the judge asked the witness whether Catherine was engaged against her will.

Theologians tried to reconcile the interests of the principals with the larger interests of their families. They argued, as theologians are wont to, without reaching a clear conclusion. On the one hand, ran the argument, children were bound to obey their parents, no matter where their own inclinations might lie. On the other hand, parents could not force their children to contract marriage "by means of threats, beatings and killings, because it is necessary that the marriage be freely consented to."[4]

Catherine Gent may have come close to committing a mortal sin by disobeying her mother, but she could not be forced to marry unless she herself consented to the union. It was her promise, pronounced in front of the Church, that prompted the accusation against her. She had accepted Martin's gift, she had promised to marry him, with witnesses present, she was, then, as good as married, unless she could prove that her promises had been obtained under duress. In a similar case, two years earlier, another orphaned girl whose hand had been sought in marriage by an older man found herself defenseless as she faced the court. The plaintiff, Gabriel Songis, had given young Marguerite a ribbon which she had accepted, thereby signifying her acceptance of his suit. In court, Marguerite resorted to the argument that she was too young to grasp the significance of the vows exchanged. The plaintiff's lawyer, however, persuaded the court that Marguerite was old enough to know what she was doing—and the judgment went against her. As the court saw it, with both her parents dead, Marguerite, who would inherit enough property so that she need not become a servant, would be best off married to Songis, whose gift she had, after all, accepted.

In view of Marguerite's reticence, the judge who handed her over to Songis may appear callous to us, but she had entered a contract and her refusal constituted a breach of promise. Besides, the circumstances were exceptional. The girl had no immediate family left and her legal guardians wanted the marriage to go ahead. The bridegroom may not have been young enough—or sufficiently handsome—to suit Marguerite, but she could hardly be left to live on her own. The insistence on free consent was not meant as a concession to the romantic longings of young girls. The principle of freedom of choice imbedded in custom and canon law was subject to a number of limitations in practice. Where political expedience or serious property interests were involved, much of the theoretical freedom of choice was eroded. Royal infants were groomed for marriage alliances practically from birth, to serve the needs of diplomacy. The children of powerful aristocratic families and the children of the very rich were not likely to resist the imperatives imposed upon their choice of marriage partners by the needs of the families involved. Ordinary people were luckier in this respect. Their right to refuse marriage partners chosen for them by their families was upheld by the Catholic Church—in part, surely, to protect the religious vocation of those who opted for celibacy and wished to join a religious order against their parents' wishes. On the other hand, preachers summoned young people to obey their parents' wishes and royal edicts specified that parents might lawfully disinherit their children if they married against their parents' wishes. A French edict of 1566, for instance, heaped abuse and threats on young people who married clandestinely "against the will of their parents and without their consent." In view of "such irreverence and ingratitude, such contempt for their fathers and mothers," the guilty parties, motivated by "lusty, indiscreet and disordered willfulness," could be legally deprived of their inheritance. Their marriages, sinful or even criminal, were, nevertheless, valid.[5]

In most cases, surely, the consent of the parents was sought and obtained. The choice of a marriage partner was certainly influenced by prudent considerations. A young man who was about to inherit the family farm was not likely to choose a landless woman—although reciprocal arrangements might allow the inheriting son to marry a girl without inheritance on the understanding that his sister would marry the inheriting brother-in-law, so that both family farms would remain undivided.[6] Marriages between those who had property and those who had none were unusual enough to suggest that young people were not often blinded by love. "A pretty face is a fool's mirror" says one of the countless proverbs warning against the attractions of mere beauty. "Never trust a starry sky or a nice arse" says a peasant proverb—and another, still, reminds us that "a pretty woman will never make you rich."[7]

While prudence played a part in the selection of marriage partners, the decision was not necessarily imposed by the families. The key decision, especially in the villages, was made by the young couple. Typically, a boy and a girl would have known each other since early childhood, although they would both be adults in their mid- or late-twenties at the time when they finally were prepared to exchange vows. Having done so, in public, their vows acquired the force of law—even if no priest was present. The eventual celebration of the wedding would serve as confirmation of an act performed months earlier. It was the engagement that counted. From that day on, the couple was presumed married.

The engagement ceremony was informal. Here is the testimony concerning the engagement of Jean Gratien to Barbe Montaigne, in the village of Moussey, in 1528. Jean walked up to Barbe and asked her, in front of several persons, whether she was married or single. She said she was single. Presumably, this question and its answer constituted some sort of improvised formality, for the record, since Jean and Barbe knew each other quite well. Then Jean said to Barbe: "Wouldn't it be better if we were married?" Barbe replied that she was willing.

"Well, then, let me engage you to each other," said one of those present.

"You don't know your ABC," said Jean. "You're the wrong person to do it." As he was speaking, Jean saw the schoolmaster coming toward them and said: "Here is the schoolmaster, he will do it well." He asked the schoolmaster to proceed with the engagement. The schoolmaster agreed to do it. He turned to Barbe and Jean and told them to exchange vows. Jean agreed. The schoolmaster took Jean's hand—and Barbe's also—and he said to Jean: "Do you promise to take her in marriage, if God and Holy Church approve, and that you will stay with her, for better or worse, until Death?"

The phrase "if God and Holy Church approve" shows up regularly in the testimony of witnesses before the bishop's court, from which this account is taken. Whether peasants and schoolmasters actually used this phrase we cannot tell. After the event, in front of the clerical court, witnesses would naturally use the phrase, to show their respect for the Church. When Jean said yes, the schoolmaster told him to kiss Barbe, to symbolize the marriage. But then someone spoke up to say that it was necessary to ask Barbe whether she consented to the exchange of vows. Barbe said she consented. Again, the schoolmaster directed Jean to kiss Barbe. He complied.

Then Jean turned to one of the witnesses, Jacques Château, and asked him to ask the bride if she was pleased. Château put the question to Barbe, to which she replied, perhaps overcome by emotion, with a silent nod. Château said: "She is pleased."[8]

Such an exchange of vows may seem casual, but it was nothing of the sort. A simple statement of acceptance, a gift exchanged, in public—these were sufficient to constitute a solemn promise as good as any written contract. Once a woman had accepted a gift, in front of witnesses, with the full understanding of what this acceptance signified, she could be sued in court if she refused to proceed with the marriage. This is precisely what happened, in 1530, to Jeanne Lepage, a flirtatious young woman from the village of Beaufort. On the occasion of a feast day, Jeanne grabbed a pin away from Jean Ragon, who was holding it in his hand.

"Give it back," said Jean. She refused.

"Well," said Jean, "since you do not want to give it back, I give it to you as a token of my intention to marry you—if God and Holy Church approve."

One of those present said to Jeanne, just to be sure there was no misunderstanding: "Jeanneton [a friendly diminutive of Jeanne], what do you say? Are you allowing yourself to be engaged to him, in full knowledge of his meaning?"

"He didn't say it well," replied Jeanne.

"Well," said Jean, "since you say I didn't say it well, let me say again that I gave you the pin as a sign of marriage. I want you to have it—if God and Holy Church approve. What more do you want of me?"

Jeanne did not reply. According to the witnesses who were to testify in court, she just laughed and pinned Jean's gift to her breast.

A hired hand who was present during this exchange was to testify in court to the effect that he heard Jean ask Jeanne what sort of *chanjon* she wanted. She was heard to say that she did not want a red one, she preferred a black one. Asked to explain what a *chanjon* was, the witness told the judge it was a belt, a special kind of belt exchanged between a bridegroom and his intended. Having heard the testimony, the court passed sentence: Jeanne was obliged to marry Jean.[9]

The exchange of vows and gifts, on the occasion of a feast day or of a country fair, involved only the principals—or need only involve the principals, as we saw, in order to have the force of law. The parents do not seem to have been directly involved. No priest need be in attendance. A man and a woman vowed to join their destinies. That was sufficient. Surely this decision was never reached lightly. The public promise must be seen as the culmination of years of waiting and prudent maneuvering. The consent of the parents, if they were living, had, no doubt, been given already, at least tacitly. In exceptional cases, when the bride was very young, her parents or legal guardians might be able to prevent her from marrying a man they did not approve of—or even force her to marry against her will. But in the majority of cases, the bride was an adult woman, close to 25 years old. In such cases, the power of the parents was limited. Some parents simply relied on their daughters' good sense, as did Julien Fleury, a Norman farmer who testified in court to this effect.

Had he forced his daughter to accept Jean Regnard as her husband? No, said the old man, he had always left it up to her, knowing that she was incapable of making a bad choice. He was aware that his daughter had been friendly with Jean Regnard for some time. Regnard was a neighbor, he had even lived in the Fleury household for some four years—and Fleury knew that "a strong friendship linked his daughter to Regnard." This friendship had reached the point where "it would be very difficult to break up without causing damage, so he was quite willing to give his consent."

Even less trusting parents found it difficult to sabotage their grown children's marriage plans. Charlotte Hotot and Nicolas Caillot, who had been seeing each other against their families' wishes, managed to overcome parental resistance in time. When the matter came before a court of law, witnesses testified to the parents' opposition. One of them, an employee of the Hotot family, testified that she had observed, over a two-year period, "an excessive familiarity between Charlotte and Nicolas, on an almost daily basis." Even though both families were very unhappy about this, "they could not prevent them from frequenting each other."

Charlotte's parents "often forbade Nicolas to come to their house, but he kept coming anyway." He was often heard to say, "that he would have her in spite of his parents and friends." Another witness told the court that Nicolas's father had often given the young man a bad time and tried to keep him from talking to Charlotte. Father and son were so much at odds "that they went for a long time without speaking to each other, even though they lived in the same house, so that, at last, the old man gave in and consented to the marriage," to avoid the trouble that might have resulted.[10]

The freedom of young people in Western Europe was altogether remarkable, when compared with the customs of other societies. The choice of a marriage partner was deeply influenced by considerations of property and inheritance, but remained an autonomous decision, a contract between consenting adults. Especially remarkable is the appearance of equality between men and women. Theologians might repeat old moral lessons about the inferiority of women, but, in practice, as we may infer from the court cases cited thus far, the exchange of vows involved men and women as equals. Instead of being handed over to her future husband, the typical rural bride exercised a choice, it would seem, as freely as did the bridegroom: she chose to accept a man, or refused him flat.

The European bride's freedom, her ease in dealing with men would have been unthinkable in other societies. Girls attended village schools together with the boys, even though bishops tried to enforce some kind of segregation.[11] Outside of school, boys and girls were free to play games together, games which rehearsed future courtship rôles, as in the case of the game of the virgin, described in eighteenth-century Burgundy.

The girl who played the part of the virgin was covered up with shirts and jackets. Surrounded by an inner circle of defending girls, the virgin was besieged by the boys who tried to get past the defenders and remove the various garments piled on top of the virgin.

"We want her in marriage," chanted the boys.

"No, no, if you marry her you will beat her," cried the girls.

But once the boys had successfully removed all the clothes piled up on top of the virgin, it was time to give in. The virgin's friends began to sing a lament for her lost youth: "Soon she will be like the rose which has lost its petals, soon she will be swallowed up, like the plum shaken from its tree." When the virgin was handed over to the victorious boys, she lamented her fate: "Alas, will you abandon me? Am I to be theirs?" she sang.

"It is your destiny," replied the girls' chorus. "You have to follow your husband. But we shall cry for you all year long, whenever we hear him beating you." At this point the virgin cried out, the boys moved in on her, surrounded her. She went down on her knees, raising her hands in supplication. The boys pretended to be moved by the pitiful sight: "Come, come, we will take better care of you than these girls in skirts who cannot defend you."

Then the virgin rose to her feet, at last—and gave her hand to the boy she liked best. She had chosen her husband, in play—and the lucky winner returned his bride to her girl friends. The game could now begin all over again.[12]

With adolescence, the games became riskier. According to a bishop, writing in 1609, the young men in his diocese visited with their girl friends on Saturday evenings—and made a point of staying so late that it would have been difficult for them to return home before morning. On this pretext, they would ask for hospitality, intending to share the girls' beds. Such requests were sanctioned by custom. The girls demanded guarantees from the boys, making them swear that nothing would happen. With the parents' approval, the couples then bedded down for the night.

Far more common were the social gatherings, on winter nights, when all the young girls of the village would come together to spin, sharing the heat and light of a single fireplace. The boys would be there, in attendance, telling stories and playing games under the supervision of the older folk. Much harmless flirting occurred on such evenings. When a girl dropped her spindle, for instance, the boys would pounce on it, confiscate it, and refuse to return it unless they got a kiss.

The ease with which boys and girls worked and played together did provoke suspicion among professional moralists, but the result of the freedom enjoyed by the young seems harmless enough. Unwanted pregnancies appear to have been exceptional. Babies born less than eight months after a wedding were few—5 percent of the total number of births recorded, usually. Even though the customary safeguards which kept premarital sex at a minimum may have broken down in the course of the eighteenth century, when some parish registers show as many as 10 percent and even 20 percent of babies born too soon after the wedding, not all these infants can be considered illegitimate. The villagers, after all, considered a couple married once they had exchanged vows. If the wedding ceremony was performed a little too late, this was no great matter. A wedding could not be improvised overnight. It was an expensive event, it required much preparation, and it had to wait until the work in the fields was done. The rhythm of the seasons dictated that certain times were best suited for celebrations of this kind. February was a good time, because there was not much work in the fields. Another good time was June, when Lent was over and when the big demands of the summer season had not yet begun.[13]

The outstanding fact to be noted about family life in early modern Europe is the late age at which men and women chose to marry. We have already had occasion to consider the consequences of delayed marriage for the size of families. A woman who waits until she is 25 years old to marry, will obviously give birth to fewer children than will a girl married at 15. Youthful marriages were the norm elsewhere in the world. In Eastern Europe, in the Balkan region or in Russia, teenage marriage was common. Samples taken from eighteenth-century Belgrade, where 92 percent of the women in the 20- to 24-year-old age group were already married, provide a sharp contrast to samples taken in rural England (18%) or Austria (20%).

The small size of Western European families—which consisted, typically, of no more than four or five persons—was guaranteed not only by the reduced number of children born to late-marrying couples—but also by the absence of the older generation from the household. This, too, may be seen as a consequence of delayed marriage. If a man waits until he is 28 to marry, he will be 29 or older before a child is born to his wife. If that child is a boy, say, and lives to reach adulthood, he will not be ready to take a wife until he, too, is 28 or thereabouts. By that time his father would be 57—and the odds of his still being alive are not good. For this reason, among others, it is rare to find more than one generation living together in a single household. In England and in the Netherlands, couples who lived with their own parents at the time when their first child was born represented, probably, no more than 5 percent of the families surveyed. The same holds true for most of France and, very likely, for most of Western Germany as well. Although local variations can be found—in the isolated, mountainous reaches of central France, for instance—the general pattern is clear enough in Western Europe, especially when compared with Eastern European samples which show large families, including grandparents, living under one roof. In the Balkans, in Hungary, Lithuania, and Russia, where some records exist for the late eighteenth century, the proportion of multi-generational families living in a single household appears to be on the order of 60 percent.

Nineteenth-century sociologists were fond of imagining that it was industrialization that had streamlined the western family. They contrasted the selfishness of the modern family with an imaginary preindustrial world in which large families were the rule. Such fancies have been destroyed by the findings of historical demographers in recent years. It seems clear now that the western family—with few children and few grandparents—was already well established long before the Industrial Revolution.[14]

The consequences of this development are several. We have already seen, in earlier chapters, that the restraint exercised by rural families acted as a safeguard against overpopulation. Refusing to establish a new family until the older generation made room for them, couples aligned their needs with fixed and scarce resources. The autonomy they achieved in this way extended to their choice of marriage partners.

An adult woman in her mid-twenties is a seasoned member of the community, not a child bride. She knows the weak points and the strengths of the eligible men in the village. She is aware of the value of her own inheritance and she can size up the bridegroom's prospects. As a veteran of the battle of the sexes, she knows how to flirt without losing her honor. Once she is ready to consider marriage, she will be seen more and more frequently in her boyfriend's company, at country fairs, at dances, on the way to local pilgrimages. When she is ready, at last, to exchange vows, she can look forward to setting up an independent household.

Up until the wedding day, single men and women remained dependents, living under their parents' authority. With marriage came independence. The old folks, if they were still living, prepared to retire. They divested themselves of their possessions in favor of the young couple, reserving only minimal rights sufficient to guarantee a decent old age. Marriage contracts often included clauses intended to safeguard the rights of a surviving parent upon retirement. The provision of meat, drink, access to the fireplace, and other domestic comforts can be found specified in such contracts. Anxious about a new daughter-in-law's attitude toward him, an old man might go so far as to make his retirement and his son's inheritance depend on the daughter-in-law's being obliging toward him. Shrewd peasants specified what should happen in the unfortunate event of incompatibility between the young couple and the surviving parents. Should an elderly lady be forced to move out, she was to receive an annual pension, consisting, for instance, of "2 bags of rye grain, 2 of millet, half a barrel of wine, a quarter of a pig, a quantity of wool and her own bed and bedding."[15]

Older men and women, if they were still alive when their grown children married, were prepared to accept a new status at this last stage of their lives. Handing over the bulk of their property to the young couple, they became sojourners—guests in their own household—free of the responsibilities implied by the management of property and dependent on their children's good will, as in the case of William King, an old Cambridgeshire farmer who testified that "his wife being dead, and his children grown up, he now liveth as a sojourner with one of his sonnes."[16]

Whether their parents were deceased or retired, a newly married couple could count on a degree of independence hard to imagine in other societies, where child brides entered a household and became subservient to their mothers-in-law, while teenage husbands deferred to their fathers. Instead of joining a clan or an extended family, the western couple, typically, began an autonomous career at the time of their marriage.

This general rule does not hold true everywhere. There were regional differences—and the pattern was not well established before the sixteenth century. In early fifteenth-century Florence, for instance—and in the countryside surrounding the great Italian city—women married at a much younger age than would become customary a century later, in France and England. In 1427, at a time when Italy had not yet recovered from the labor shortage caused by the plague, it was still common for Florentine girls to marry at 16. The men, however, would normally be ten years older than their brides. Even so, they did not always acquire the independence from the older generation which generally came at the time of marriage a century later in much of Western Europe. Perhaps as many as half of the newly married Florentine men continued, for some time, to live under the authority of their fathers in the fifteenth century. In other respects, the Florentine family already exhibited the traits characteristic of later times: households were small, the older generation was not usually present, and sisters, brothers, aunts, or uncles were rarely found living under the same roof.[17]

Even in fourteenth-century Italy, relations between young wives and mature husbands appear surprisingly balanced. The private correspondence of the merchant Francesco Datini, reveals the respect he showed toward his wife Margherita, even though she had been no older than 16 or 18 when he married her. Datini himself had lived very freely before he proposed to Margherita at the age of 40—and he continued to live freely afterwards. His friends knew him as "a man who kept women and lived only on partridges, adoring art and money, and forgetting the Creator and himself." That is to say that Datini's bachelor life hardly corresponded to the misery imagined by popular preachers, who spoke of the wifeless man as a brute beast who "lies in a ditch, and when he has put a sheet on his bed, he never takes it off again, until it is torn. And in the room in which he eats, the floor is covered with a melon rind and bones and salad leaves."

Datini was a self-made man. His parents were killed by the plague in 1348. Soon after his fifteenth birthday, he sold a small piece of land, part of his modest inheritance, and went off to Avignon where he made his fortune dealing in arms, in currency, and in luxury objects. When Datini proposed to Margherita, whom he took without a dowry, he seemed ready to settle down. The chief preoccupation of this by now middle-aged man was to have legitimate heirs. Unfortunately, Margherita proved incapable of bearing him a child. Their relationship was embittered by this misfortune. Datini stayed away for years at a time, maintaining separate establishments in Pisa or in Florence, while Margherita remained in Prato, supervising the household.

The letters exchanged between husband and wife, over the years, are not free of strain. Margherita knew perfectly well that old Francesco had serving maids and slave girls warming his bed, while she had to settle for the lonely life of the stay-at-home wife and business partner. Yet, in spite of the disparity in age—and in spite of Margherita's failure to produce an heir—Datini's letters show that he was not entirely an overbearing husband.

Away from home, he complained about his wife's absence—but not so strongly as to induce her to join him.

"I eat nothing that pleases me," he complains to Margherita. "If you were here, I would be more at ease."

"It seems to me," replies Margherita, "that it would please you to have me there with the whole household, and yet you leave the choice to me. This you do of your courtesy, and I am not worthy of so much honor. I have resolved to go, not only to Pisa, but to the ends of the earth, if it should please you."

Nothing came of these intentions. Datini was busy making money and caressing his concubines, while Margherita was needed to supervise affairs at home. The old man kept sending her detailed instructions. "Tomorrow morning," he would write, "send back the branches of dried raisins and the bread . . . and send the barrel of vinegar . . . remember to wash the mule's feet with hot water, down to her hoofs and have her well fed and cared for. And have my hose made . . . and give some of the millet that is left to the nag, and see that it is well mashed . . . and speed the sale of the two barrels of wine in Belli's house; and empty all the other vats in the cellar, the ones with white wine, that have already been opened."

On another day he sends his laundry list, together with 30 herrings, a sack of capers and 20 pounds of flour and peas. Margherita was to send him 50 oranges "in such a manner that they are not spoiled," 25 loaves of bread, two barrels of oil and a bushel of grain. "And remember to do all you have to do," he adds, nagging, "and look well to the barrels and feed the beasts well, and every evening shut the door well and look to the light and see to it that I shall not have to scold."

But Francesco was not the only one capable of scolding. "You bid me make merry and be of good cheer," writes Margherita. "I have nothing in the world to make me merry. You could do so if you would, but you will not."

On the subject of her husband's infidelities, Margherita could find sharp words: "I believe no word you write. On every other matter I would take my oath that you would never tell a lie; but as to your keeping a w . . . . . , as to this, I would vow that you never spoke the truth."

Francesco tried to placate her with soft words: "Never have you been so joyful . . . as you will be on my return," he promised. And he added in a most conciliatory manner: "It has pleased God to soften my heart about many things which used to grieve you—and you were right, and I never said you were not."

"As to your making peace with me," replied Margherita, as combative as ever, "I am glad: for I was never at war with you. I know not what gift you will bring me; that I cannot understand, but when I get it I will thank you. You are not in the habit of bringing me too many gifts when you come home."

The bickering that went on between Francesco and Margherita caused comments among their friends.

"Verily, I eat roast chestnuts every morning before I set forth," boasts one of Datini's cronies. "But that is because my wife pampers me, as I do her. Not like you, who are always wrangling with yours."

Another writes that he thought "there are some secrets between you, which you will not have bandied in other men's mouths. Well, go with God. I live more simply with my Francesca, and what her will is, is mine too."

Margherita was capable of acknowledging her husband's prerogatives as master of the household in such a way that he was forced to back down: "As to your staying away," she wrote, "you can do as you please, being our master, which is a fine office, but should be used with discretion. I am fully disposed to live together, as God wills . . . and I am in the right, and you will not change it by shouting!"

Francesco replied meekly: "When you come here, and hear from all men concerning my behavior, you will be satisfied." And he signed, sheepishly, "Francesco . . . with much grief on many accounts, owing to my failure in many things."[18]

The examples cited here are not meant to suggest that husbands and wives looked upon each other as equals. It was generally understood that the man of the household was also the master. Husbands who failed to control their wives risked being mocked in public, especially during the noisy charades and games at Carnival time. In spite of these fairly universal assumptions, women in Western Europe enjoyed a position found nowhere else. They could choose or refuse husbands, they could remarry freely after their husband's death, they could inherit property, they could work. Not only were they granted power over the affairs of the household, but they were also able to work for wages and to run a business.[19]

Nothing would have struck a visitor from the Muslim world more powerfully than the freedom of western women who moved about in the streets, their faces uncovered, their behavior bold. Instead of being confined to a family compound, European women were never segregated. Denied access to the professions associated with the Church—the priesthood, law, medicine—women of all conditions did have access to elementary education at least, even though this development did not have the unqualified approval of Church authorities. It is difficult to say whether Signora Datini's ability to write letters was unusual in fourteenth-century Italy—or whether little Ginevra, the child born to Datini's slave Lucia, was exceptionally favored when she was taught to read. In sixteenth-century France, in any case, village schools enrolling girls as well as boys were entirely commonplace.[20]

Taken as a group, women always show up far behind men, whenever attempts are made to calculate the proportion of those who could read and write, just as women always come far behind in the wages they were able to command. The usual measure of literacy—namely, the ability of brides and bridegrooms to sign their names to marriage contracts—always reveals a disproportion between men and women. In a small, semirural town in central France, for instance, this method of measuring literacy produces a figure of 35 percent for men and 27 percent for women, in the seventeenth century.[21]

There are difficulties inherent in this method, to be sure. We shall never agree on a satisfactory definition of literacy, let alone calculate precisely the number of men and women who could read. What we can say with assurance is that girls were not systematically excluded from schooling. Even in rural communities, public schoolmasters were almost always available and children of both sexes were encouraged to attend school. If a village could not afford to hire a separate schoolmistress for the girls, the schoolmaster would take them together with the boys. Often, the school-master's wife was willing to teach the girls.

A characteristic arrangement of this kind is sought by the schoolmaster Chaussenc, in September 1593, when he writes to the elected admin-istrators of a village in the Rhône Valley: "I hear that your schoolmaster is leaving, so I write to you to let you know that I am willing to serve you and teach your boys good habits, reading in Latin and in French, and all sorts of letters."

Aware of his limitations, Master Chaussenc admits that he does not know too much about Latin grammar, but he is proud of his writing skills: "If you find my handwriting acceptable, of which this letter may serve as a sample, although I can do better, you will find that I will serve you as loyally as any man of letters could, without tormenting your children."

As for the girls, Chaussenc has a proposition in mind: "If you have girls that need teaching, for reading, writing and good habits, I have a wife who is not staying with me at the moment but whom I can send for and who is as good at this work as any that can be found in the entire province."[22]

Although women were less frequently literate than men, what is really significant is that schooling was not a mysterious activity reserved for boys who would become priests, as it was in most other societies and as it had been, not so long ago, in Europe also. To read and write in French, in Italian, in English, German, Dutch, or Spanish was a practical skill, useful to anyone. Its cultivation was openly encouraged. Orphaned boys and girls cared for in municipal poorhouses were taught to read and write, in the hope of improving their chances for future employment. The children of peasants were encouraged to come to school very early in the morning—or else, while still very young, before they were strong enough to be of much use in the fields.[23] The proportion of those who acquired mastery in these skills may have been low, by twentieth-century stan-dards, but it was remarkable and unprecedented.[24] Literacy, in early modern Europe, was not linked to membership in the priestly estate. It was linked, quite clearly, to property. A large sample taken from deposi-tions made in the consistory court of an English diocese between 1580 and 1700, establishes this connection firmly. On the evidence of this sample, there were hardly any illiterates in the upper—that is, wealthier— reaches of English society. Even among substantial farmers of the yeoman class, only 35 percent were illiterate. Among tradesmen and craftsmen, 44 percent. A closer look at the tradesmen and craftsmen in this sample shows that some occupations were linked to high levels of literacy, while others were not. Merchants were generally literate. Only 6 percent of the grocers failed to sign, and only 9 percent of the haberdashers. Bakers, tanners, and innkeepers did less well, but still included a comfortable majority of men able to sign. Weavers, glovemakers, tailors did not do too badly. But those whose work consisted almost entirely of manual labor outdoors had an appalling record: 76 percent of the masons, 88 percent of the bricklayers, 90 percent of the shepherds, and 97 percent of the thatchers were illiterate.[25]

Such samples—and the figures they produce—are to be used with caution. They can serve to confirm the less precise impressions historians inevitably gather in the course of their work in sixteenth- and seven- teenth-century archives. One cannot fail to come away from these massive collections of papers without the conviction that this was a society only partly literate in the aggregate, but almost totally literate in certain sectors of urban life. While women generally lagged behind, they were not excluded from schooling and we may suspect that the distance that separated a shepherd, in his thinking, from a merchant or a judge, was far greater than that which separated a woman from her husband.

X

WORLDLY MINDS

The existence of public schools in early modern Europe, beginning in the fourteenth century and reaching something like a saturation point in the sixteenth, is an index of this society's worldliness. Monasteries and cathedrals still took in boys to be trained for the priesthood, but the new public schools served another function. At the elementary level, they taught basic literacy in the language of everyday, in French or in German, not in Latin, the language of the Church. In this sense, the public schools may be considered as useless for future priests. Protestant pastors required training in the Biblical languages—Latin, Greek, even Hebrew—as much as their Catholic counterparts. The municipal elementary schools taught none of these subjects. Their clientele consisted of the sons and daughters of ordinary people, of children who were not destined for clerical careers.

What was the purpose of teaching ordinary laymen, even women, to read and write in their own language? One could argue that such simple learning was bound to strengthen lay piety—and this was indeed the argument made in Protestant lands and, somewhat later and more reluctantly, in Catholic regions too. But the argument was made after the fact. Catholic authorities, in particular, were ever mindful of the dangers inherent in easy access to learning. Both government officials and leaders of the Roman Church could be heard expressing their misgivings about the proliferation of public schools, of which, in Cardinal Richelieu's view, there were far too many, "even in the smallest towns of the kingdom."

"It is the ease of access to this bewildering number of schools that has enabled the meanest artisans to send their children to these schools, where they are taught free of charge—and that is what has ruined everything," declared French bishops.

What was being ruined? The objection to free public schools was twofold: book learning was said to entice the sons of workingmen away from useful occupations such as farming, and it was suspected of promoting undesirable attitudes. Answering these objections, the trustees of an eighteenth-century municipal school conceded that "other schools teach book learning, thus deflecting the children from useful skills. As a result, the state is losing useful subjects. Their studies take them away from their fathers' occupations." Their own school, they claimed, avoided these dangers by concentrating on the teaching of "the elements of religion, reading, writing and arithmetic" only, while encouraging "that spirit of religion and hard-working honesty that is the mark of the citizen useful to the state, instead of pandering to that spirit of idleness, arrogance and irreligion that is so costly and dangerous to society."[1]

It is this spirit of "arrogance and irreligion" that is the subject of this chapter. Both Catholic and Protestant church leaders made every effort to control what was going on in the public schools. The churches hoped to eliminate schooling that was not directly answerable to bishops and other guardians of orthodoxy. The Catholic clergy automatically detected signs of heresy in laymen who taught school. Inquisitors occasionally descended on suspect schools. Some teachers were denounced, arrested, and burned in public squares. Religious orders were mobilized to replace laymen in the schools. In Protestant regions pastors sought the backing of the state to impose orthodoxy in the schools. But there was a limit to the kind of thought control envisioned by enthusiastic clergymen. It was one thing to keep an eye on Latin grammar schools located in sizeable cities. It was another to dream of censoring the multitude of modest schools found in small towns and villages. Even further removed from the reach of officials was the whole world of informal learning propagated by improvised tutors and teachers and kept going, spontaneously, by obscure individuals who needed only a book or two to get started on the road to "arrogance."

Take the case of Thomas Tryon, the son of a village tiler and plasterer, born in 1634, whose experience with formal schooling had been inconclusive, at first. "About five years old," Thomas tells us, "I was put to school, but, being addicted to play, after the example of my young schoolfellows, I scarcely learnt to distinguish my Letters, before I was taken away to work for my living." At the age of thirteen, Thomas could not read. But then, "thinking of the vast usefulness of Reading, I bought me a Primer, and got now one, then another, to teach me to spell, and so learned to Read imperfectly, my teachers themselves not being ready Readers: But in a little time having learn't to Read competently well, I was desirous to learn to Write, but was at a great loss for a Master, none of my Fellow-Shepherds being able to teach me. At last I bethought myself of a lame young Man who taught some poor People's Children to Read and Write; and having by this time got two Sheep of my own, I applied myself to him, and agreed with him to give him one of my sheep to teach me to make the Letters, and Joyn them together."[2] Thomas Tryon gave up the shepherd's life and went off to London to apprentice himself to a printer. He was to found his own religious sect, eventually, thus confirming that reading could indeed become a subversive activity when practiced, without supervision, by ordinary people.

The best-known case of a self-taught peasant that has come to light so far is the remarkable story of Domenico Scandella, born in 1532 in the Italian village of Montereale. Domenico earned his living as a "miller, carpenter, sawyer, mason and other things." He was a respectable member of the village community. He was married and he had children. Although he claimed to be poor, his income from two flour mills that he rented and from two fields that he worked was sufficient to enable him to provide his daughters with adequate dowries—and he was well established in the village which he served as mayor in 1581.

Domenico, who may have attended a public school in a neighboring village, definitely knew how to read, write, and add. On September 28, 1583, he was denounced to the Holy Office of the Inquisition. The record of his interrogations gives us a rare opportunity to meet an ordinary peasant and to hear him talking freely about almost everything.[3]

Domenico stood accused of having uttered "heretical and most impious words"—not once, or twice, but continually and for many years.

"He is always arguing with somebody about the faith, just for the sake of arguing, even with the priest," testified one witness.

"He will argue with anyone," said another, "and when he started to debate with me I said to him: I am a shoemaker and you a miller, and you are not an educated man, so what's the use of talking about it?"

Domenico did not have much use for priests. "Priests want us under their thumb," he would say, "just to keep us quiet, while they have a good time." As for him, he knew God better than they did. He expressed doubts about the virginity of Mary. He had been heard saying that Masses for the dead were useless.

"What are you doing giving alms in memory of these few ashes?" he had asked a neighbor. When questioned about this, Domenico explained that he meant "that we should be concerned about helping each other while we are still in this world."

Domenico objected to the wealth of the clergy. "The pope, cardinals and bishops are so great and rich that everything belongs to the Church and to the priests and they oppress the poor."

Domenico's understanding of religion required no priests. "I would want us to believe in the majesty of God, to be good and to do as Jesus Christ commanded when he replied to those Jews who questioned him about what law was to be kept: love God and your neighbor."

Furthermore, Domenico believed that all creatures were equally dear to God. "Christians, heretics, Turks or Jews are all saved in the same manner," he said.

He rejected all the sacraments, including baptism, as human inventions, as "merchandise" in the hands of the clergy. "I believe that the law and commandments of the Church are all a matter of business and they make their living from this."

He was of the opinion that "You might as well go and confess to a tree as to priests and monks." As for communion, he said: "I do not see anything but a single piece of dough, how can this be our Lord God? And what is God anyway? Nothing but earth, water and air."

Even the Bible did not escape Domenico's criticism: "I believe that Sacred Scripture was given by God, but was afterward added to by men. Only four words would suffice in this Holy Scripture."

Domenico had no need for organized religion. "I do not want anything else but to do good," he said.

Domenico Scandella was not a visionary, he was not a rebel or an outcast, he was not a member of a secret sect. He was a respected citizen of Montereale—and he had been making these surprising statements openly, for many years. When questioned by the Inquisitor, his neighbors and relatives were obviously not going to admit that they had listened approvingly, all along, to the talk of a suspected heretic. But they did say that they liked Domenico very much, that he was an honorable man, and that he was everybody's friend. Had it not been for an anonymous denunciation, Domenico would have lived out the last years of his life without coming to the attention of the authorities—and we would never have heard of him.

Domenico insisted on the originality of his ideas. He had not been influenced by anyone, he claimed. He had read some books which he had bought or borrowed, but the conclusions he drew from his reading were his own.

Among those who lent books to Domenico were the village priest, a woman in a nearby village, and a cousin of his. All the same, said

Domenico, "I have never met anyone who holds my opinions. My opinions come out of my head."

Domenico's natural curiosity and his philosophical turn of mind were sharpened by a lifetime of debating. He was as contentious as a theologian. It may be true that Domenico never met anyone who held opinions quite like his own, but he was acquainted with a certain Nicola, a painter by trade, who had a reputation as "a great heretic" and from whom he borrowed a copy of Boccaccio's *Decameron,* one of the books from which he drew his opinions. Although he may have reached most of his opinions on his own, something the Inquisitor found hard to believe, there are, nevertheless, connections between Domenico's views and those embraced openly in regions the Inquisition could not reach.

"If I did not have to fear the sword of justice," admitted Domenico, "I would amaze everyone with my talk."

Amazing talk had been heard for close to a century, wherever the Church had lost its grip on the sword of justice. In England, in Germany, in France, in Holland—wherever governments permitted attacks against the Roman doctrine—the Pope was compared to the Devil, priests and monks were vilified as greedy traffickers in "merchandise," masses for the dead, as well as the adoration of relics were rejected as categorically as Domenico was to express himself.

"As for their relics, such as an arm, a body, a head, a hand or a leg," said he, "I believe that they are like ours when they are dead, and we should not adore them. We should not adore their images, but God alone, who created heaven and earth."

Domenico's angry outbursts against priests and monks would have been perfectly acceptable in Protestant countries. "You priests and monks," he said, "you too want to know more than God, and you are like the devil, and you want to become Gods on earth, and know as much as God."

Domenico believed that "the spirit of God dwells in all of us," and, also, that "anyone who has studied can become a priest without being ordained," a point of view accepted by many people in regions from which the Roman clergy had recently retreated. Domenico's rejection of confession, too, was a perfectly acceptable opinion in Protestant lands. Instead of confessing to priests, he thought, men should confess "to the majesty of God in their hearts, and beseech him to forgive their sins."

Some of Domenico's opinions were commonly held even in Catholic regions, although the Church fought against them. Marriage, for instance, was not something, in Domenico's view, that God had established. It was an arrangement, he believed, that had been invented by human beings—and there had been a time when "a man and a woman would exchange vows, and this sufficed."

No need to go to Protestant countries for confirmation of this belief. Shortly before Domenico was executed, a Spanish archbishop complained about the customs of the peasants in his own archdiocese. "Wives have been given to the husbands . . . before they had exchanged the marriage vows in church." On pain of excommunication, the archbishop ordered that the contracting parties "shall not take any oaths nor marry themselves with future promises nor celebrate with friends and kinfolk, meats and repasts, nor any other rejoicings or feasts until they shall have been married by the vows," but this order seems to have had little effect.[4]

Some of Domenico's opinions were so far out of line that he might have gotten into trouble anywhere, not just in Montereale. He did not have much confidence in the Bible, nor did he believe in Hell. In spite of that, he considered himself a good Christian. "I am a baptized Christian," he wrote, "and have always lived in a Christian way, and have always performed Christian works, and I have always been obedient to my superiors and to my spiritual fathers, to the best of my power—and, always, morning and night, I crossed myself with the sign of the Cross— *et sempre matina et sera io son segnato col segno de la santa croze.*"

The parish priest of Montereale agreed: Domenico Scandella was "Christian and orthodox," he explained, "if the internal can be judged by the external."[5] What did it mean to be a Christian, then, in 1583? Was it possible to judge private beliefs on the evidence of outward behavior? From the perspective of the professionals of salvation, being a Christian required the understanding of certain fundamental beliefs—and unwavering acceptance of the Church's teachings. Using such a test, honest churchmen would have been driven to despair had they insisted on probing beyond the level of outward observances. It was best not to be too fastidious. Making the sign of the cross, morning and night; cutting a cross at knife-point in the crust of a loaf of bread about to be eaten; wearing silver or wooden crosses around their necks, millions of men and women thought of themselves as Christians. They went on pilgrimages when the fancy seized them, they left small offerings at various shrines, they came to Church on Sundays, and they buried their dead in consecrated ground. At the same time, they avoided confession, they participated only with great reluctance in the performance of their religious duties, they knew almost nothing of the basic teachings of their Church— and they did not trust priests.

Whenever bishops began quizzing parishioners on such subjects as the meaning of the Trinity or, even, on the wording of the most common prayers, they discovered abysmal ignorance. In a Catholic diocese, in 1542, the vicar-general noted coldly that "experience teaches us that there are married persons in the diocese, husbands as well as wives, who have children they ought to be instructing in the Catholic faith, but are so ignorant that they do not know their prayers and they live, so to speak, like beasts." This kind of observation could have been made almost everywhere, in Catholic as well as in Protestant lands. In spite of the missionary zeal which prompted sporadic campaigns of indoctrination, the results were meager. Nor is it always clear whether the clergy preferred an enlightened laity, familiar with doctrine, but given to debating and capable of suspect thoughts—or an ignorant laity safe from such temptations.[6]

Domenico Scandella was hardly alone in pursuing his curiosity and in his implacable contempt for priests. The tortured body of the old miller had hardly been disposed of when a report reached the Inquisitor's office, to the effect that "there was a certain man named Marco, or perhaps Marcato, who believed that when a body died, the soul also died with it."[7]

In spite of the Inquisitor's efforts to link Domenico's "heretical and impious words" with the teaching of the Lutherans, is is clear that materialist and skeptical opinions could arise quite independently of any formal teaching in the minds of laymen.

The records kept by bishop Fournier, in the course of repeated inquiries into the opinions of the inhabitants of the village of Montaillou, in the foothills of the Pyrénées, between 1318 and 1325, show the full dimensions of disaffection from official doctrines. Even though Fournier took it for granted, as did the priests who interrogated Domenico Scandella, that a simple peasant could not come up with dangerous ideas on his own— and that he was therefore, inevitably, the victim of outside agitators, of confirmed and organized heretics—this point of view is hard to maintain in the face of the witnesses' testimony.

In Montaillou there were, in fact, heretic missionaries. But the men and women rounded up by the Inquisitor's armed auxiliaries often held views that were no more compatible with the doctrines of the heretics than with those of the Catholics.

Some merely pleaded ignorance: "I do not know what the fast days of the Church are, apart from Lent and Friday," said a shepherd.

Another villager's refusal to fast was founded on his contempt for official observances. "For five weeks during Lent I ate meat," he admitted. "I could have abstained from doing so without physical risk." At the time, his brother, outraged by his forbidden meat eating, said to him: "If you're not careful, I'll fling your plate of meat all over you."

Heretic missionaries encouraged the peasants of Montaillou in their resistance to the Church. "The priests do not do their duty," they said. "They do not instruct their flock as they should and all they do is eat the grass that belongs to their sheep."

The villagers, however, needed no prompting to notice the weaknesses and faults of the Catholic priest. Nor were they overly impressed by the heretic missionaries either. Bertrand Cordier was talking to an acquaintance of his, Arnaud.

"What's new?" asked Arnaud.

"They say the Antichrist is born," reported Bertrand. "Everyone must put his soul in order. The end of the world is near."

"I don't believe it," replied Arnaud calmly. "The world has neither beginning nor end. Let's go to bed."

To the Inquisitor, who pointed out to him that his beliefs were not in accord with the Church's teaching, Arnaud replied that he lacked religious instruction: "Because of my work in the stone quarries," he explained, "I have to leave Mass very early and I do not have the time to hear the sermons." It would seem that Arnaud's views were not uncommon. "I have heard many of the people say that the world always existed and always would exist in the future," Arnaud told the Inquisitor.

Another villager, Jaquette, was overheard talking to some of her friends at the mill, saying: "There is no other age but our own."

Such notions as the Creation, the Last Judgment, life after death, and resurrection met with fairly general skepticism, judging from the Inquisitor's report. One villager, watching a heap of bones being pulled out of a newly dug grave, said: "How is it possible for the souls of the Dead to come back one day in the same bones as were theirs before?"

Another went further. Raymond, of the village of Tignac, believed that the soul consisted merely of blood—and disappeared after death. He denied the Resurrection. As for Heaven, in his opinion, that was when you were happy in this world. Hell was when you were miserable, and that was all. He had no use for bishops who, he said, had been brought into this world like everyone else "by fucking and shitting." In the village square, in front of witnesses, Raymond asserted that Christ, too, was created "through fucking and shitting, rocking back and forth and fucking . . . just like the rest of us." Needless to say, Raymond did not believe in the virginity of Mary, he denied Christ's crucifixion, Resurrection, and Ascension—and he did not, of course, believe in communion.

"God and the Virgin Mary," he thought, "were nothing else but this visible and audible world."[8]

Were these exceptional cases? No doubt they were. They were certainly exceptional in the sense that they belong to the rare category of cases involving direct testimony given by peasants. There is no way of guessing whether the independence of mind found in Montereale or in Montaillou was common elsewhere. At least, the researches of Professors Ginzburg and Le Roy Ladurie open our eyes to the inadequacy of the official point of view regarding the beliefs of ordinary people.

Bishops—and other agents of official culture—tended to regard peasants as little more than beasts who—if they were heard to express strange or subtle opinions—could only be echoing thoughts inspired by heretics. The people was seen by its masters as a "great mass of lead that neither sees nor hears." The evidence we have reviewed so far leads in another direction altogether. It suggests that peasants who had little formal schooling knew enough to see priests as parasitical accomplices of the mighty who despoiled them.[9]

Hatred of the clergy was deeply rooted. Only fear kept laymen from speaking up. Wherever secular authorities broke with the Church and allowed anticlerical agitation to flourish, entire provinces went over to the Protestant cause overnight, and with considerable enthusiasm—an enthusiasm that lasted only such time as it took to realize that Lutheran or Calvinist ministers were no more inclined to protect the peasants' interests than was the Catholic Church.

Criticism of the clergy was spontaneous and it was to be found almost everywhere, in one form or another. Working people were likely to stress the greed and laziness of priests who took their tithes and gave little in return, living, or so it seemed, a life of ease.

"Go out and glean, it's good weather. Learn how to work, you fine merchants, you've eaten too long without doing anything," shouted the crowd at a fair in Normandy, in the summer of 1561. The historian who reports these taunts directed at Catholic priests is quick to conclude that "the language of Protestant pamphlets . . . was becoming the language of the crowd as well."[10]

Was there really any need to read Protestant pamphlets to become resentful of the privileges enjoyed by the clergy? Those angry insults shouted at the fairgrounds were not newly invented. The very words used in 1561 were heard thirty years earlier, in a small town, hundreds of kilometers to the south, when no pamphlets circulated and Protestantism did not yet have an organized form in France: "Get to work, you priests," shouted a student. "Soon you will have to start digging in the vineyards."[11]

Examples of this sort could be cited endlessly. Already in the early years of the fourteenth century, the dissidents of Montaillou complained about the greed and the corruption of the Church.

"The Pope devours the blood and sweat of the poor. And the bishops and the priests, who are rich and honored and self-indulgent, behave in the same manner. Whereas St. Peter abandoned his wife, his children, his fields, his vineyards and his possessions to follow Christ," said a peasant of Montaillou.

As for the Franciscan and Dominican friars, their vows of poverty and chastity did not impress the peasants of Montaillou. "They go to the houses of rich, young and beautiful women. They take their money and, if they consent, they sleep carnally with them, putting on appearances of humility the while."

A shepherd, asked to give his opinion of the preaching friars, gave it freely: "Instead of saving the souls of the dead and sending them to Heaven, they gorge themselves at banquets, after funerals. And do you think that their great houses were built by the labor of their own hands? No, these friars, they are wicked wolves! They would like to devour us all, dead or alive."[12]

Spoken by believers or by skeptics, heard in village squares—or read in books and pamphlets—such words were common enough to find their way into schoolbooks, as in the case of the *Colloquies* of Erasmus. The instant popularity of Protestant criticism of the Roman clergy makes sense only if one understands how deeply laymen resented the clergy. They resented its wealth, they hated tithing, they had no use for the traffic in pardons and indulgences, and they were suspicious of the ideal of clerical celibacy professed by men and women whose carnal instincts, they surmised, were as highly developed as were their own.

Catholic historians have tended to blame such disaffection on the ineffectiveness of parish priests—or else, on heretic propaganda. Protestant historians, for their part, are inclined to imagine that critics and opponents of the Roman clergy were bound to be forerunners of the evangelical reformers, yearning for the day when the Gospel would be preached at last. And yet, it seems that even when the clergy was reformed, laymen continued to resist indoctrination.

In Catholic lands, when ignorant priests were replaced with competent ones, and heretics were disposed of, the peasantry continued to ignore the teaching of the Church. In Lutheran Germany, once Catholic priests had been driven out, to be replaced by well-trained Lutheran ministers, no significant improvement was to result. The "dumb people" *(das dumme Volk)*—in the contemptuous words of Protestant leaders—still refused to cooperate.

Sixteenth- and seventeenth-century records of inspection tours undertaken by Lutheran officials present a picture of mass disaffection no different from the hostility to priests found in Catholic regions. Both Catholic and Protestant officials were routinely scandalized by the religious indifference of ordinary people, which they attributed to ignorance and to natural wickedness. These explanations are not very convincing.

More to the point are the statements of the peasants themselves, recorded in testimony given during inspection tours and analyzed by Professor Gerald Strauss.[13] The peasants' own testimony shows that they were not, on the whole, very interested in religious doctrine. If they were, for the most part, ignorant of even the most elementary points of Christian teaching, it was not because they were "a crude, ignorant folk, and untaught." Most of the villages surveyed by Lutheran officials did in fact have schoolmasters. Even though the children attended school, and even though reasonably competent ministers preached in the parish churches, the villagers, when questioned, could not give satisfactory answers.

"They know nothing of Christianity," concludes one report. "Great carelessness hereabouts toward the Gospel," adds another. "People make no secret of their scorn for the Sunday catechism and the Friday sermon," we hear elsewhere. As Professor Strauss observes, people simply stayed away from church.

"No one wants to go to church," reports a pastor. "Not a soul comes during the week . . . and on Sundays they usually stay away without having obtained permission."

When they do come to church, they "jump up and make for the door" as soon as the minister begins to preach. Village after village displays its gross ignorance of Christian doctrine to the visiting officials. In one village, not even the Church elders could remember any of the Ten Commandments. In another, the inhabitants do not know "who their Redeemer and Savior is." In a district in which nearly every village had a school, few of the children—and even fewer adults—were capable of reciting the catechism. One pastor admitted that he had simply given up on religious instruction "because people here pay so little attention to it."

Lutheran pastors exclaimed over their parishioners' mind-boggling ignorance, but they knew that they were not dealing with dumb brutes. It was only when it came to religion that laymen displayed stubborn unconcern.

"You cannot make them go to church, no matter what you say. To worldly affairs," on the other hand, notes one observer, "they turn with a passion." It was only "for the Church that they have no time and no interest."

When a cloth merchant was asked whether he could remember the topic of the previous Sunday's sermon, he replied that he could remember nothing at all. What about the price of wool as it stood one year ago? To that question the merchant replied immediately and with great accuracy. Well, then, he was asked, why was it that he could remember wool prices so well—and sermons not at all?

"Wool is my business," replied the merchant. "I must think about it day and night, for I can't make a living without it. As for the sermon and the catechism, I don't need them so much."

In spite of pressure from the authorities—and in spite of the efforts made by presumably zealous clergymen—the mass of the population kept resisting indoctrination. This was true of Lutheran Saxony as well as of Catholic Bavaria—and it was true in the cities as well as in the countryside. The bishop of Salzburg may have found comfort in ascribing doctrinal ignorance to the "common man" only—that creature who could not even "say the Lord's Prayer or the Ave Maria"—but other officials were not blind to the fact that religious indifference was not limited to peasants.

"In many places of your Grace's realm," they complained, "the common people, following the example of nobles and burghers, show a flagrant contempt for the servants of God's work." His Grace responded by issuing official decrees to make "people desist at long last from showing such frightening ingratitude toward God." Predictably, such decrees had little effect: "daily experience tells us, alas, that few of our people have taken the Gospel to heart."

The Lutheran church visitation records reveal an overwhelming and stubborn resistance to churchgoing. What was the cause of this obstinate refusal? Why was there so much "contempt for the servants of God's work"? The pastors spoke of laziness and vice.

"Most of them are gruesome epicureans," says one report, meaning that the villagers cared only to eat and drink and had no interest in the salvation of their souls. "We have found epicureans here who hardly know a word of the catechism and never think about their salvation. Indeed, several have let it be known that it's all the same to them whether we bury them in the churchyard or elsewhere."

When the villagers were asked why they did not come to hear the pastors' Sunday sermons, they were capable of replying that "the Turk and the Pope are not doing us any harm"—that is to say that they had no interest in the topics favored by the preachers who denounced the Roman Pope and distant infidels. The themes of official propaganda were of no concern to the villagers.

Resistance to churchgoing was by no means universal. In many Catholic regions, Sunday services were well attended. But this does not necessarily mean that villagers came to be edified and instructed by the priests. Sunday services provided an excuse for various festivities. Not particularly interested in the sacraments, the Catholic laity took pleasure in banquets and processions. The priest often remained an outsider whose influence on his parishioners remained marginal. Ignorant of most of the basic tenets of the official faith, Catholic villagers were in the habit of constructing their own religion, a rather practical religion. They made vows to saints without the intervention of priests. They favored local shrines and they chose to venerate saints in a spirit hardly compatible with orthodox teaching.

Spanish peasants viewed their favorite saints as consultants, so to speak, whose services they were prepared to reward with vigils and processions. Their concerns were worldly. They worried about crops and they made offerings to saints who could protect their investment. When hail damaged their vineyards, they turned to St. Anne, if it was on St. Anne's day that the hail had fallen. St. Gregory was considered an effective pesticide. When they were not sure which saint to turn to, they organized a lottery to help them in their choice. Lighting 12 separate candles, each of which represented a particular saint, they chose the one whose candle burned the longest. The saint's duty, once chosen as the parish's *abogado* (advocate) was to "plead to God for this place."[14]

Viewed from the perspective of the nineteenth and twentieth centuries, the religious behavior of the majority in earlier times may appear as remarkably conformist. Everybody was a Christian in the sixteenth century, even Domenico Scandella. Everyone lived in constant proximity to crucifixes. Church bells tolled in every village. In their outward behavior, most people paid obeisance to the requirements of the churches, at least in a minimal way.

At the same time, we cannot ignore the chorus of complaints produced by priests and ministers who were deeply suspicious of the laity. The safest course in any assessment of the religious life of Europeans is to distinguish between the various and fierce orthodoxies propounded in the pulpits, on the one hand, and, on the other, the private beliefs and the public behavior of the laity, which rarely matched the zeal of the clergy.

When the French revolutionary government came close to abolishing Christianity altogether, in the 1790s, masses of people joined in a general attack on priests, smashing religious statuary, and turning churches into stables and warehouses. Is this kind of anticlerical violence conceivable without a long apprenticeship? Is it enough to point to a decline in religious commitment throughout the eighteenth century?[15] Or should one seek the sources of irreligion in the more distant past, when indifference, as shown in the visitation records of the sixteenth and seventeenth centuries, was already common? Explanations of religious indifference which stress the ignorance of peasants and the pernicious effects of libertinism among the educated classes may suit the needs of clerical propaganda, but the phenomenon is too deeply rooted in the past to be explained in this fashion. A more useful line of inquiry is provided by Professor Pierre Chaunu, who argues that European society was already remarkably secular in the fourteenth century, when compared to the rest of the world.[16]

XI

CONCLUSION

In any case, to speak of religious indifference is to adopt the language of bishops. It would be imprudent to accept definitions of orthodoxy coming from such quarters. We cannot conclude, from the testimony of diocesan visitations or from isolated cases of peasants questioned by inquisitors, that the mass of the population was hostile to religion. All we can surmise is that ordinary people often distrusted the clergy and that they were less concerned with officially approved religious practices than they were with local and private manifestations of the religious impulse.

The religion of the people varied from one locality to the next. It could express itself in ways that struck bishops as blasphemous. The materialism of some of the peasants of Montaillou, the skepticism of the miller of Montereale, the revolutionary interpretation given to the Gospel by the followers of Thomas Müntzer, or, for that matter, the long, secret history of the veneration of a holy dog[1]—these are but some examples of the distance which could separate the mass of the laity from the official agents of tithe-collecting churches backed by the sword of justice.

For this reason I have not thought it useful to enter into the tortuous history of the Lutheran, Calvinist, or Catholic reformations. These movements produced spiritual leaders, zealots, and martyrs as well as legions of opportunists. There were moments when peasants and artisans persuaded themselves, briefly, that a doctor of theology had taken up their cause. But what the artisans of Memmingen and Meaux saw in the Gospel was different from what Luther or Lefevre had in mind.[2] Where ordinary people saw liberation from worldly oppression, the doctors of theology saw spiritual liberation only.

Such costly misunderstandings do offer clues to the social changes experienced by the mass of Western Europeans. The antagonism between the clergy and the laity may be understood, at least in part, as incomprehension resulting from the confrontation of two distinct world views. That of the clergy was cast in the mold of a late antique social order, while that of the laity, to the extent that its outlook could be independent of clerical culture, reflected newer realities. Attitudes toward authority, work, women, commerce, or celibacy, for instance, provide test cases of this conflict between an ancient culture, preserved in the museum of clerical tradition, and a newer one, born of the experience of the medieval commune.

The quarrel with the Church found expression in the heretical movements of the fourteenth and fifteenth centuries and in the establishment of Protestant churches in the sixteenth century. It continued until the clergy, even in Catholic states, lost many of its privileges and was subordinated to secular authorities. For this was the issue which inflamed popular feelings: let priests be like ordinary men, subject to the same laws; let them perform their duties, let them become accountable to the community which taxes itself to pay their wages. Priests ceased to be viewed as privileged members of a mysterious caste. They were seen, increasingly, as specialized professional men, akin to lawyers and physicians, whose training the community had invested capital in and from whose presumed expertise the community expected a reasonable return.

Priests, together with knights and princes, were part of the inheritance from an earlier civilization. From the fourteenth century onward, this inheritance was gradually reinterpreted so as to fit into a social order no longer entirely legitimized by appeals to divine dispensation. The clergy may well have been among the earliest victims of the newer standards used to assess ancient privileges and powers. The nobility was not far behind. And monarchs themselves, their powers swelled beyond recognition by their newfound ability to tax their subjects, were to discover that those who pay the piper also develop an inclination to call the tune. Medieval élites and medieval institutions were forced to adapt to a society which was rapidly changing.

We ought to resist the temptation to define the changes in question in such a way as to suit the needs of the written page, the lecture hall, the single, sweeping formula. The conclusions offered here are meant only as a partial summation of those aspects of social change discussed in the preceding chapters. With that caution in mind, it may be useful to point to the importance of property.

Property had been an extremely nebulous concept in medieval society. We cannot be far off the mark if we assume that it was the establishment of urban, market-oriented communes, beginning in the eleventh century, that set in motion the slow development which was to transform the western world. A rural, servile society led by warrior chieftains, inheritors of ancient regalia, allowed itself to be molded into a new shape by merchants and artisans whose power rested on the possession of private property alone. The kind of property associated with late-medieval urban dwellers did not resemble the collection of rights enjoyed by feudal seigneurs. Instead of being limited to the exaction of customary labor services in the fields, the newer kind of property rights extended to every conceivable form of human activity. Coins were minted, new forms of credit were invented, land as well as labor joined a market economy, eventually, within which everything of value—all property and all services—was to be, increasingly, defined by contract and valued according to the shifting relationship between supply and demand. This trend was to suffer no setbacks. Neither wars nor epidemics could stay its course. Moralists complained about the insidious effects of money, peasants rebelled against the pressures of a rudimentary capitalism, clerics thundered against usury—all in vain.

Serfdom disappeared because one cannot do business with serfs. Eventually, dukes and princes would disappear for the same reason. Meanwhile, rural production was adapted to the needs of a market economy—only in part, to be sure, but deeply enough so as to introduce the uncertainties, the turmoil, and the rough justice of the marketplace into village society. Rural output was harnessed to urban needs. Cash crops, where this was a profitable option, crowded out subsistence farming. Spanish wool, Burgundian wine, Dutch dairy products were among the goods singled out as suitable for the long-distance trade. Peasants lost land and became wage laborers, their energy redirected, in part, to the production of goods other than farm products. Mining, construction, deep sea fishing, textile production, as well as military service, were some of the activities that absorbed wage earners from the rural sector. The consequence of these changes in the western economy, which had become acutely visible by the early sixteenth century, was to introduce an element of fluidity into this society—and this may not have been sufficiently emphasized in this book.

My chief purpose, after all, has been to single out those features of early modern society in Western Europe which changed so slowly that they may appear permanent—visible as early as the fourteenth century in some cases, fully developed by 1600, and still in place a century later. In stressing these lasting aspects, we run the risk of losing sight of the movement that was one of the main characteristics of early modern society: this was a world which embraced change, even while denying that change was occurring.

The impression of a society which transforms itself daily is inseparable from the importance of private property, of business, of profit in the lives of a growing proportion of its members. Among the urban communes of the thirteenth century, there were already gigantic commercial centers such as Genoa, in which even ordinary people were caught up in the fever of risk-taking.[3] The astonishing successes of the western economy, its ability to harness capital, to develop new markets, to lie in wait for every conceivable exotic product that might sell—anything from cotton and paper to artichokes, tobacco, sugar, or potatoes—is not directly part of our story.[4] But it stands to reason that the sensational innovations, commercial and technological both, that marked the early history of capitalism cannot be viewed as accidental. They can be understood only as the result of a mental outlook developed in western cities and absent elsewhere—absent, or too weak to overcome the resistance of political, social, and cultural inhibitions against the primacy of the pursuit of profit in human relations.

Western cities were business partnerships to begin with, and they never stopped being just that, even as they grew in complexity, even as they reached their various accommodations with prelates, princes, lords, and peasants. Instead of succumbing to the influence of rural, clerical, or dynastic imperatives, these cities, on the whole, succeeded in subverting the older components of European society, infecting lord and peasant, priest and king alike, with their own drive for rational, calculating profit strategies.

In time, seigneurial domains were transformed into real estate and the Church became a corporation subservient to its bankers. Charismatic chieftains were tamed by financiers until they began to resemble chief executive officers worried over their budgets. Peasants learned to calculate, weighing the advantages of legal freedom and of family-size limitation. Even when their crops failed and their debts were called in, western peasants were not always and everywhere defeated by destiny. Often they turned out to be adaptable enough to impose their will on the land, draining swamps and shifting to new crops.[5] If opportunity beckoned in the nearby town, nothing stood in the way of the enterprising peasant who set off for the city—where his descendants might well appear, some day, on the honor rolls of the history of capitalism.

From the Rhineland to the Tagus River valley, from the Catalan shores to the delta of the Po, wherever the cargoes of sailing ships and barges were unloaded, men and women hitched their destinies to the propelling force of a vigorous capitalism, blind to sentiment, but equally impervious to the claims of blood, lineage, tradition, or prophecy. Surviving portraits of Renaissance businessmen attest to their sober outlook, even when they are shown wearing cardinals' hats. These chiseled faces with bold expressions and probing eyes are the true monuments of our past.

NOTES

PREFACE

1. Lucien Febvre's *Philippe II et la Franche Comté* (Paris, 1912), has not been translated into English. The journal *Annales E.S.C.* is available in any university library. For a full account of the origins of the *Annales*, see George Huppert, "Storia e scienze sociali: Bloch, Febvre e le prime *Annales*" in *Il Mondo Contemporaneo*, X (La Nuova Italia, Torino, 1983).

2. Professor Heinz Schilling, however, observes a new interest in social history among his Dutch colleagues. See Heinz Schilling, "Calvinistische Presbyterien in Städten der Frühneuzeit," in Wilfried Ehbrecht, ed., *Städtische Führungsgruppen und Gemeinde in der werdenden Neuzeit* (Köln, 1980), 385–444, note 73 a, p. 405, and references to the results of S. Hart's investigations on literacy [*Geschriften Getal* (Dordrecht, 1976)], in Heinz Schilling, "Die Geschichte der nördlichen Niederlande und die Modernisierungstheorie," in Reinhart Kosellek, ed., *Wandel und Beharrung in der Frühen Neuzeit* [Geschichte und Gesellschaft 8 (1982), 475–517, p. 479, note 8].

I

1. Gérard Bouchard, *Le village immobile* (Paris, 1972).

2. For these estimates, see Pierre Chaunu and Richard Gascon, *Histoire économique et sociale de la France*, I, 1 (Paris, 1977), 177–216.

3. Ibid., 32–33.

II

1. The phrase, from the writings of Cellorigo, a lawyer from Vallodolid, is cited by Bartolomé Bennassar, who uses it as the concluding sentence of his splendid book, *Valladolid au siècle d'or* (Paris, 1967), 573.

2. That at least ⅓ of a peasant's harvest is given up in the form of tithes, taxes, fees, and interest payments, of which bourgeois receive the lion's share, is well established. For a recent summary of what is known, see Roger Chartier, Guy Chaussinand-Nogaret, Hugues Neveux, Emmanuel Le Roy Ladurie, and Bernard Quilliet, *Histoire de la France urbaine*, III (Paris, 1981).

3. Evidence summed up in Bernard Chevalier's *Les bonnes villes de France* (Paris, 1982), 180–184. A good example of urban stocking is provided by the French city of Reims where 60% of the households had cellars and attics filled with food in 1422.

4. Lucien Febvre, *Life in Renaissance France* (Cambridge, Mass., 1979).

5. See Arlette Farge, *Le vol d'aliments* (Paris, 1974).

6. This process is made abundantly clear in David Herlihy and Christiane Klapisch-Zuber, *Les Toscans et leurs familles* (Paris, 1978). The city of Florence contains only 14% of the population of Tuscany, but ⅓ of Tuscany's wealth is concentrated in Florence. The authors sum the process up aptly: "Florence, like a star surrounded by less brilliant planets, the small towns of Tuscany, shines in the black world of the destitute rural areas" (249).

7. Cited in J. K. Hyde, *Society and Politics in Medieval Italy* (London, 1973).
8. See the excellent description of the fortifications of Nürnberg in Gerald Strauss, *Nuremberg in the Sixteenth Century* (Bloomington, Indiana, 1976).
9. Hyde, *Society and Politics in Medieval Italy.*
10. See Pierre Chaunu and Richard Gascon, *Histoire économique et sociale de la France*, I (Paris, 1977), 27–32.
11. French government statistics simply use the figure of 2,000 inhabitants as a cut-off point: anything below that is a village, anything above a city. See Chevalier, *Bonnes villes*, 21.
12. For the fundamentally different character of Muslim, Chinese, or Japanese urban centers, see Ira M. Lapidus, *Muslim Cities* (Cambridge, Mass., 1967); Mark Elvin, "Chinese Cities" in P. Abrams and E. A. Wrigley, eds., *Towns in Societies* (Cambridge, England, 1978); and John W. Hall, "The Castle Town and Japan's Modern Urbanization" in *Studies in the Institutional History of Early Modern Japan* (Princeton, 1968).
13. See Jean Delumeau, *Rome au XVIᵉ siècle* (Paris, 1975).
14. Strauss, *Nuremberg*, and Bennassar, *Valladolid.*
15. Bennassar, *Valladolid*, gives the proportion of the poor in Valladolid, in 1561, as 9.54%–634 households out of a total of 6,644. In Segovia, the proportion is 15.74%.
16. The laws concerning citizenship requirements for those who were not born within the walls are fairly standard. The requirements in Nördlingen may serve as an illustration: The candidate had to demonstrate that he owned an adequate amount of property and that his skills as an artisan or merchant were satisfactory; he had to pay a fee; and he remained on probation for 5 years. See Christopher R. Friedrichs, *Urban Society in an Age of War* (Princeton, 1979), 40.
17. The figures for Coventry are likely to be fairly standard: 24.8%. In the French city of Reims, a little earlier, the number is close to that. See Charles Pythian-Adams, *Desolation of a City* (Cambridge, England, 1979), 204.
18. The knight and lady quoted here are fictional characters appearing in the well-known twelfth-century poem *Perceval*. Cited by Professor Jacques Le Goff in his introduction to *Histoire de la France urbaine*, II (Paris, 1980).
19. Cited by Pierre Chaunu, *La civilisation de l'Europe classique* (Paris, 1966), 317.
20. Pierre Goubert, *Beauvais et le Beauvaisis de 1600 à 1730 (Paris, 1960).* I am using the abridged edition, *Cent mille provinciaux au XVIIᵉ siècle* (Paris, 1968).
21. On exorcising insects, see William A. Christian, Jr., *Local Religion in 16th Century Spain* (Princeton, 1981). For a good illustration of peasant attitudes toward poor harvests, consider the peasant who was accused of heresy for having said: "Old man God is too old, he does not know what he is doing anymore. He spoils everything. Our vineyards and our pear orchards are lost. We'll have to make another God." Cited by J. Roserot de Melin, *Antonio Carracciolo* (Paris, 1923), 194.
22. On Valladolid grain purchases, Bennassar, *Valladolid*, 67; on Valencia, see Henri Lapeyre, "L'organisation municipale de la ville de Valence," in *Villes de l'Europe Méditerrannéenne*, Actes du Colloque de Nice (Paris, 1969), 127–137.

III

1. See Fernand Braudel, *Civilisation matérielle, économie et capitalisme.* 3 vols. (Paris, 1979).
2. See Strauss, *Nuremberg.*

3. Michel de Montaigne, *Essais* (Paris: Gallimard, 1962), "Des cannibales," pp. 212–213.

4. Charles Pythian-Adams, *Desolation of a City* (Cambridge, 1979), 79.

5. Ibid., 95.

6. Ibid., 99–124.

7. Ibid., 74–79.

8. For a recent account of the formal rivalries between Sienese wards, see Alan Dundes and Alessandro Falassi, *La Terra in Piazza* (Berkeley, 1975).

9. For the discussion of sexual frustration and prostitution here, I am indebted to the fine study by Jacques Rossiaud, "Prostitution, jeunesse et société dans les villes du sud-est de la France au 15e siècle," *Annales E.S.C. 31* (1978), 289–325.

10. Quoted by Natalie Z. Davis, *Society and Culture in Early Modern France* (Stanford, 1975), 97–123.

IV

1. The spokesman of the city council, addressing the commoners of Frankfurt. Cited by Gerald L. Soliday, *A Community in Conflict* (Hanover, N.H., 1974), 69.

2. Christopher R. Friedrichs, *Urban Society in an Age of War: Nördlingen, 1580–1720* (Princeton, 1979).

3. The preceding analysis is founded on Professor Soliday's study of Frankfurt (*A Community in Conflict*).

4. See Bennassar, *Valladolid*.

5. See George Huppert, *Les Bourgeois gentilshommes* (Chicago, 1977).

6. Huppert, *Bourgeois gentilshommes*, 88.

7. Ibid., 31.

8. Ibid., 47.

9. I owe this reference to Professor Henry Heller of the University of Manitoba.

10. See Huppert, *Bourgeois gentilshommes*.

V

1. Quoted by Emmanuel Le Roy Ladurie, *Montaillou* (New York, 1979), 21 and 261.

2. Jean Meyer, *La noblesse bretonne* (Paris, 1972), 285, 291.

3. Lawrence Stone, *The Crisis of the English Aristocracy* (Oxford, 1965), 109.

4. Meyer, *Noblesse*, 37.

5. Goubert, *Beauvais*, 241.

6. Pierre Goubert, "Société traditionnelle et société nouvelle," in F. Braudel and E. Labrousse, eds., *Histoire économique et sociale de la France*, II (Paris, 1970), 607.

7. Meyer, *Noblesse*, 50.

8. Ibid., 251.

9. Stone, *Aristocracy*, 41. See also Henry Kamen, *The Iron Century* (N.Y., 1972), 163.

10. Gaston Roupnel, *La ville et la campagne au 17e siècle* (Paris, 1955), 127–133.

11. Meyer, *Noblesse*, 29.

12. W. H. Lewis, *The Splendid Century* (New York, 1957), 39–44.

13. Meyer, *Noblesse*, 302.
14. Roupnel, *La ville*, 163.
15. See Huppert, *Bourgeois gentilshommes*.
16. Emmanuel Le Roy Ladurie, *Carnival in Romans* (N.Y., 1979), 347.
17. Stone, *Aristocracy*, 18, 22, 23.

VI

1. Isabelle Guérin, *La vie rurale en Sologne aux 14ᵉ et 15ᵉ siècles* (Paris, 1960), 212.
2. Ibid., 228.
3. See Jean Pierre Gutton, *La sociabilité villageoise dans l'ancienne France* (Paris, 1979).
4. Michael R. Weisser, *The Peasants of the Montes* (Chicago, 1976), 38–44.
5. Anne Zink, *Azereix* (Paris, 1969), 200.
6. Quoted by Noël Salomon, *La campagne de la Nouvelle Castille à la fin du 16ᵉ siècle* (Paris, 1964).
7. Goubert, *Beauvais*, 184.
8. Ibid., 214.
9. For examples of this process in action, see Guy Cabourdin, *Terre et hommes en Lorraine (1560–1635)*. 2 vols. (Nancy, 1977); Paul Raveau, *L'agriculture et les classes paysannes* (Paris, 1926); Yvonne Bézard, *La vie rurale dans le sud de la région parisienne, 1450–1560* (Paris, 1929); Marc Venard, *Bourgeois et paysans au 17ᵉ siècle* (Paris, 1957); Huppert, *Bourgeois gentilshommes*.
10. See Emmanuel Le Roy Ladurie, *The Peasants of Languedoc* (Urbana, 1974).
11. See Domenico Sella, *Crisis and Continuity: The Economy of Spanish Lombardy in the 17th Century* (Cambridge, Mass., 1979).
12. This was the conclusion of Pierre de St. Jacob, in his classic *Les paysans de la Bourgogne du nord* (Paris, 1960).
13. For the schoolmasters of Azereix, see Zink, *Azereix*, 212. The literature on village schoolmasters in France is enormous. For references, see Huppert, *Public Schools*.
14. On the decline of literacy in Azereix, see Zink, *Azereix*, 254.
15. Weisser, *Montes*.

VII

1. Jean Delumeau, *La peur en Occident* (Paris, 1978), 143.
2. Henry Kamen, *The Iron Century* (New York, 1972), 336, 352.
3. The standard—and classic—work on the German Peasants' War is Günther Franz, *Der Deutsche Bauernkrieg*, first published in 1933, which I am using in its 8th edition (Darmstadt, 1969). In these pages I have taken advantage of the most recent research, as summarized in Buszello, Blickle and Endres, eds., *Der Deutsche Bauernkrieg*. UTB (Paderborn: Schöningh, 1984). Within this collaborative work, I have relied especially on Rudolf Endres' discussion of the revolt in Franconia (135–139) and for the events in Mühlhausen (157–164); on Horst Buszello's analysis of the rebellion's goals (281–296); on Peter Blickle's summary of the impact of printed pamphlets (54); and on the analysis of the consequences of the rebellion by Helmut Gabel and Winfried Schulze (324). I am much obliged to Professors Endres, Schulze, and Blickle, in particular, for the help they gave me in the course of informal discussions surrounding the symposium organized by the Historisches Kolleg in Munich, in June 1985.
4. Kamen, *Iron Century*, 347–348.

5. Ibid., 331–332.

6. For a detailed analysis of this revolt, see Madeleine Foisil, *La révolte des Nu-Pieds* (Paris, 1970).

7. *Carnaval de Romans* (Paris, 1979). References are to the English language edition, *Carnival in Romans* (New York, 1979).

8. A classic example is that of the great study of French rebellions by the Soviet historian Boris Porchnev, *Les soulèvements populaires en France de 1623 à 1648* (Paris, 1963). See Porchnev's analysis of peasant motivation, *inter alia*, on page 280.

9. Cited by Sal Alexander Westrich, *The Ormée of Bordeaux* (Baltimore, 1972), 40.

10. Ibid.

11. Ibid., 40–59.

VIII

1. Bartolomé Bennassar, *Valladolid au siècle d'or* (Paris, 1967), 436; Olwen Hufton, *The Poor of Eighteenth Century France* (Oxford, 1974), 24; and O. Hufton, *Bayeux in the Late Eighteenth Century* (Oxford, 1967), 86–87.

2. Bennassar, *Valladolid*, 437.

3. Hufton, *Poor*, 176.

4. Ibid., 23.

5. Ibid., 116.

6. Bennassar, *Valladolid*, 542. This estimate is based on a survey of all babies baptized in 14 parishes of the city over a six-year period, 1592–97. The total number of baptisms was 7,086. During this six-year period, 688 abandoned infants were recorded in the city.

7. Claude Delasselle, "Abandoned Children in 18th Century Paris," in Forster and Ranum, eds., *Deviants and the Abandoned in French Society* (Baltimore, 1978).

8. Hufton, *Poor*, 27–30.

9. Bennassar, *Valladolid*, 445–446.

10. Iris Origo, "The Domestic Enemy," *Speculum* XXX (1955), 321–366.

11. Bennassar, *Valladolid*, 443.

12. Hufton, *Poor*, 84–85.

13. Ibid., 25.

14. This case, one among many, is cited by Bronislaw Geremek, *Les marginaux parisiens aux 14e et 15e siècles* (Paris, 1976), 126–134.

15. Hufton, *Poor*, 209.

16. Jean Delumeau, *Rome au 16e siècle* (Paris, 1975), 97.

17. Hufton, *Poor*, 253.

18. Andre Zysberg, "Galley Rowers in the Mid-Eighteenth Century," in Forster and Ranum, eds., *Deviants*, 94.

19. André Abbiateci, "Arsonists in Eighteenth Century France," in Forster and Ranum, eds., *Deviants*, 164–168.

20. Hufton, *Poor*, 271–272 and 268-269.

21. Kamen, *Iron Century*, 343–345.

22. Zysberg, in *Deviants*, 172.

23. See Jacques Louis Ménétra, *Journal de ma vie*, edited and introduced by Daniel Roche. (Paris, 1982).

24. Charles Verlinden, *L'esclavage dans l'Europe médiévale*. 2 vols. (Bruges, 1955). See especially I, 843.

25. Origo, "Domestic Enemy," 334.

26. Ibid., 332, 334.
27. Ibid., 343ff.
28. Iris Origo, *The Merchant of Prato* (New York, 1957), 177, 198–199.
29. Ibid., 207.
30. Ibid., 210.
31. Cited by Verlinden, *Esclavage*, I, 843.

IX

1. Bennassar, *Valladolid*, 409.
2. Weisser, *Montes*, 78–80.
3. Jean Louis Flandrin, *Les amours paysannes* (Paris, 1975), 53–55.
4. Ibid., 40.
5. Ibid., 53, 42.
6. See Zink, *Azereix*.
7. Flandrin, *Amours*, 130.
8. Ibid., 182.
9. Ibid., 112.
10. Ibid., 98.
11. Huppert, *Public Schools*.
12. Flandrin, *Amours*.
13. Ibid., 123, 121, 179.
14. For a recent summary, see Michael Mitterauer and Reinhard Sieder, *The European Family* (Chicago, 1982).
15. Cited by Zink, *Azereix*.
16. Margaret Spufford, "Peasant Inheritance Customs and Land Distribution in Cambridgeshire from the 16th to the 18th Centuries," in Goody, Thirsk, and Thompson, eds., *Family and Inheritance* (Cambridge, 1976), 174.
17. Klapisch and Herlihy, *Les Toscans et leurs familles* (Paris, 1978), 404, 490.
18. Origo, *Merchant of Prato*, 165–182.
19. On working women, see Natalie Z. Davis, *Culture and Society*, 70.
20. Huppert, *Public Schools*, 132–133, and *Bourgeois gentilshommes*, 68–70.
21. Huppert, *Public Schools*, 130.
22. Ibid., 132–133.
23. Ibid.
24. In the French city of Caen, in the eighteenth century, nine men out of ten could sign their names—and seven women out of ten. Nothing even faintly resembling such competence could be found outside of Western Europe. (See Jean Claude Perrot, *Genèse d'une ville moderne: Caen au 18ᵉ siècle*. 2 vols. (Paris, 1975), I, 309.
25. David Cressy, "Levels of Illiteracy in England, 1530–1730," in Harvey J. Graff, ed., *Literacy and Social Development in the West: A Reader* (Cambridge, 1981), 108.

X

1. Huppert, *Public Schools*, 128.
2. Margaret Spufford, "First Steps in Literacy: The Reading and Writing Experiences of the Humblest Seventeenth Century Spiritual Autobiographers," in Graff, *Literacy*, 132.
3. See Carlo Ginzburg, *The Cheese and the Worms* (Baltimore, 1980).
4. Cited by Carmelo Lison-Tolosana, *Belmonte de los caballeros* (Oxford, 1966).

5. Ginzburg, *Cheese*, 87.

6. Pierre Chaunu, *Eglise, culture et société* (Paris, 1981), 431.

7. Ginzburg, *Cheese*, 128.

8. Emmanuel Le Roy Ladurie, *Montaillou* (N.Y., 1979), 306–326.

9. Chaunu, *Eglise*, 427, citing the case of the diocese of Avignon, confirms this exploitation.

10. Philip Benedict, *Rouen During the Wars of Religion* (Cambridge, 1981), 56.

11. See Fallières and Durengues, eds., "Enquête sur les commencements du protestantisme en Agenais," *Recueil des travaux de la société d'agriculture d'Agen*, 16 (1913), 213–386.

12. Le Roy Ladurie, *Montaillou*, 333.

13. Gerald Strauss, *Luther's House of Learning* (Baltimore, 1978).

14. William Christian, *Local Religion in Sixteenth Century Spain* (Princeton, 1981).

15. John McManners, *Death in the Enlightenment* (Oxford, 1981).

16. Pierre Chaunu, *Le temps des réformes* (Paris, 1975).

XI

1. For this curious story, see the fascinating study, recently translated from the French, by Jean Claude Schmitt, *The Holy Greyhound* (N.Y., 1983).

2. On the artisans of Meaux, see Henry Heller, *The Conquest of Poverty: The Calvinist Revolt in Sixteenth Century France* (Leiden: Brill, 1986).

3. Best introduction to this phenomenon, Robert Lopez, "The Trade of Medieval Europe: the South," in *Cambridge Economic History of Europe*, 6 vols. (Cambridge, 1952), II.

4. For this, see Fernand Braudel, *Civilisation matérielle, économie et capitalisme, XVe–XVIIIe siècles*. 3 vols. (Paris, 1979), now available in English translation.

5. The clearest case of peasant adaptation to a capitalist economy is to be seen in Holland. For this see Jan de Vries, *The Dutch Rural Economy in the Golden Age* (New Haven, 1974).

BIBLIOGRAPHICAL ESSAY

The following suggestions for further reading are addressed to two different kinds of readers. On the one hand, to casual readers, who might wish merely to read another book or two; such readers will find a selection of readily available books in English here. On the other hand, to students who might have the time and the inclination to pursue some topic in a fairly systematic way. For the convenience of this second kind of reader, there is a sampling, here, of the literature in French as well as in English. However, this bibliographical essay is not to be confused with a thorough bibliography. For one thing, only book titles are listed here, even though much of the specialized literature is to be found in periodicals.

The most practical way to get a bibliographical orientation is to browse through the pages of the French journal *Annales E.S.C.,* which acts as the international clearing house for social history. Even readers who do not have a good command of the French language will find it useful to collect at least the titles of the books and articles reviewed in *Annales* in the past 30 years. The brief book reviews in the *American Historical Review,* while in no sense authoritative, can also provide a bibliographical orientation. The British journal *Past and Present,* which does not publish book reviews, is the liveliest and the most consistently intelligent periodical concerned with social history in the English language. Browsing through its volumes, one can get a good idea of what is important in this field.

The closest thing to a general, European-wide treatment of early modern social history in English is Henry Kamen's *The Iron Century* (N.Y., 1972), which covers the late 16th and early 17th centuries only; a new paperback edition of this book is now available from Hutchinson under the title, *European Society, 1500–1700* (London, 1984). Also from Hutchinson, and also in paperback, there is Sheldon J. Watts's *Social History of Western Europe* (Hutchinson University Library for Africa. London, 1984), which is concerned with the rural population of Western Europe, 1450–1720. The book was written for use in African universities, which gives it an unusual perspective.

In French, there are several collaborative works, limited to France alone, but superbly conceived. Of these, I recommend F. Braudel and E. Labrousse, eds., *Histoire économique et sociale de la France* (Paris, 1970), II; and Roger Chartier, Guy Chaussinand-Nogaret, Hugues Neveux, Emmanuel Le Roy Ladurie, and Bernard Quilliet, *Histoire de la France urbaine* (Paris, 1981), III.

The history of population is a field in itself. For an introduction, see T. H. Hollingsworth, *Historical Demography* (London, 1969). Also E. A. Wrigley, ed., *An Introduction to English Historical Demography* (London, 1966); and the same, *Population and History* (London, 1969). Also J. Goody, J. Thirsk, and E. P. Thompson, eds., *Family and Inheritance: Rural Society in Western Europe, 1200–1800* (Cambridge, 1976); L. Stone, *The Family, Sex and Marriage in England, 1500–1800* (N.Y., 1977); Peter Laslett, *The World We Have Lost* (London, 1965); Richard Wall, ed., *Family Forms in Historical Europe* (Cambridge, 1983); D. V. Glass and E. D. Eversley, eds., *Population in History* (London, 1965); Michael Mitterauer and Reinhard Siedel, *The European Family* (Chicago, 1982); and Jean Louis Flandrin, *Families in Former Times* (Cambridge, 1979). For more specific studies, outside of England, see the pioneering monographs by Louis Henry, *Anciennes familles Genevoises* (Paris, 1956); and by Louis Henry and Etienne Gautier, *La population de Crulai* (Paris, 1958); J. Nadal, *La population catalane, 1353–1717* (Paris, 1960); and E. Baratier, *La démographie provençale du 13ᵉ au 16ᵉ siècles* (Paris, 1961).

Among the more recent studies: François Lebrun, *Les hommes et la mort en Anjou* (Paris, 1971); the same, *La vie conjugale sous l'ancien régime* (Paris, 1975); Alain Croix, *Nantes au 16ᵉ siècle* (Paris, 1974); A. Higounet-Nadal, *Perigueux aux 14ᵉ et 15ᵉ siècles* (Bordeaux, 1978); Christiane Klapisch-Zuber and David Herlihy, *Les Toscans et leurs familles* (Paris, 1978), now in English, *The Tuscans and Their Families* (New Haven, Conn., 1985); and J. N. Biraben, *Les hommes et la peste en France et dans les pays européens*, 2 vols. (Paris, 1975–1976).

Most social historians focus on a single village or city. Among the few regional studies in English: Domenico Sella, *Crisis and Continuity: the economy of Spanish Lombardy in the 17th century* (Cambridge, Mass., 1979), which is only incidentally concerned with social history. The same is true of Jan de Vries, *The Dutch Rural Economy in the Golden Age* (New Haven, 1974). For England, there are regional studies by C. W. Chalklin, *Seventeenth Century Kent* (London, 1965); and by S. J. Watts, *Northumberland* (Leicester, 1975).

Among the French regional studies, the pioneering work by Lucien Febvre, *Philippe II et la Franche Comté* (Paris, 1912), is at the origin of a number of other ambitious regional studies, including R. Latouche, *La Vie en Bas Quercy* (Toulouse, 1923); Gaston Roupnel, *La ville et la campagne* (Paris, 1922), on Burgundy in the 17th century; and Henri Drouot, *Mayenne et la Bourgogne* (Paris, 1937). Fernand Braudel's *La méditerrannée et le monde méditerrannéen à l'époque de Philippe II* (Paris, 1949), directly inspired by Febvre's *Franche Comté*, is a justly celebrated work whose second, revised edition (Paris, 1966) is also available in English translation. Pierre Goubert's *Beauvais et le Beauvaisis* (Paris, 1960) and Emmanuel Le Roy Ladurie's *Les paysans de Languedoc*, 2 vols. (Paris, 1966)—the latter available in an abridged English translation—are among the best examples of social history done in the *Annales* tradition and incorporating techniques not available to the previous generation of historians.

Rural society at the local level is best studied in the periodical literature, especially through *Annales E.S.C.*, which misses nothing of importance and can serve as a sure guide to the innumerable village monographs published in many languages since 1929. For a sampling of this enormous literature in English: Norman and Ethel Gras, *The Economic and Social History of an English Village* (Cambridge, Mass., 1930); Mildred Campbell, *The English Yeoman under Elizabeth and the Early Stuarts* (New Haven, 1942); W. G. Hoskins, *The Midland Peasant* (London, 1957); Margaret Spufford, *Contrasting Communities: English Villagers in the 16th and 17th Centuries* (N.Y., 1974); Michael Weisser, *The Peasants of the Montes* (Chicago, 1976); Thomas Shepperd, *Lourmarin in the 18th Century* (Baltimore, 1971); and Emmanuel Le Roy Ladurie, *Montaillou* (N.Y., 1978).

Good examples of French village monographs not available in translation are Gérard Bouchard, *Le village immobile* (Paris, 1972); and Anne Zink, *Azereix* (Paris, 1969).

For urban history, we have a number of studies in English, including Olwen Hufton, *Bayeux in the 18th Century* (Oxford, 1968); Gerald Strauss, *Nuremberg in the Sixteenth Century* (N.Y., 1966); Gerald Soliday, *A Community in Conflict* (Hanover, N.H., 1974), on Frankfurt; Christopher Friedrichs, *Urban Society in an Age of War* (Princeton, 1979), on Nördlingen; Charles Pythian-Adams, *Desolation of a City* (Cambridge, 1979), on Coventry; Philip Benedict, *Rouen during the Wars of Religion* (Princeton, 1981); Thomas Brady, *Ruling Class, Régime and Reformation at Strasbourg, 1520–1555* (Leiden, 1978); Ronald Weissman, *Ritual Brotherhood in Renaissance Florence* (N.Y., 1982); Edward Muir, *Civic Ritual in Renaissance Venice* (Princeton, 1981); Samuel Cohn, *The Laboring Classes in Renaissance Florence* (N.Y., 1980); F. W. Kent, *Neighbours and Neighbourhood in Renaissance Florence* (N.Y., 1982); and Barbara Diefendorf, *Paris City Councillors in the Sixteenth Century* (Princeton, 1982).

Among the French urban studies which served as models for the more recent English and American monographs, one should mention, in addition to Pierre Goubert's *Beauvais* (1960), at least the following:

Jacques Heers, *Gênes au 15e siècle* (Paris, 1961)
Bartolomé Bennassar, *Valladolid au siècle d'or* (Paris, 1967)
Pierre Deyon, *Amiens* (Paris, 1967)
Marcel Couturier, *Structures sociales à Châteaudun* (Paris, 1969)
Maurice Garden, *Lyon et les lyonnais au 18e siècle* (Paris, 1970)
Richard Gascon, *Grand commerce et vie urbaine au 16e siècle* (Paris, 1971), on Lyon

An excellent all around introduction to French urban history for the earlier period—up to the sixteenth century—is provided by Bernard Chevalier in his *Les bonnes villes de France* (Paris, 1982).

For special aspects of French urban life, the following are available in English: Emmanuel Le Roy Ladurie, *Carnival in Romans* (N.Y., 1979); Natalie Z. Davis, *Society and Culture in Early Modern France* (Stanford, 1975), a collection of previously published essays; Philip Hoffman, *Church and Community in the Diocese of Lyon* (New Haven, 1984); and George Huppert, *Public Schools in Renaissance France* (Urbana, 1984).

There are few book-length studies, in English, of the aristocracy. Lawrence Stone's *Crisis of the Aristocracy* (Oxford, 1965), (England only) stands out. See also J. C. Davis, *The Decline of the Venetian Nobility* (Baltimore, 1962); Vivian Gruder, *The Royal Provincial Intendants* (Ithaca, 1968); Peter Burke, *Venice and Amsterdam* (London, 1974); Ruth Pike, *Aristocrats and Traders* (N.Y., 1972), on Seville; Robert Forster, *The House of the Saulx-Tavannes* (Baltimore, 1970); George Huppert, *Les Bourgeois Gentilshommes: An essay on the definition of élites in Renaissance France* (Chicago, 1977); Robert Harding, *Anatomy of a Power Elite* (New Haven, 1978), on French provincial governors as a group.

In French, one of the more thorough studies of a provincial aristocracy is Jean Meyer, *La noblesse Bretonne* (Paris, 1966). See also Jean-Marie Constant, *Nobles et paysans en Beauce* (Lille, 1981); and Jean Nicholas, *La Savoie au 18e siècle: noblesse et bourgeoisie*, 2 vols. (Paris, 1978).

On the poor, see Olwen Hufton, *The Poor of Eighteenth Century France* (Oxford, 1974); and Jeffry Kaplow, *The Names of Kings: the Parisian Laboring Poor in the 18th Century* (N.Y., 1972). In French, Michel Mollat, *Etudes sur l'histoire de la pauvreté*, 2 vols. (Paris, 1974); Jean Pierre Gutton, *La société et les pauvres* (Paris, 1972); and Bronislaw Geremek, *Les marginaux parisiens* (Paris, 1975).

On religion and popular culture, a number of significant studies in English: Keith Thomas, *Religion and the Decline of Magic* (London, 1971); Gerald Strauss, *Luther's House of Learning* (Baltimore, 1978); A. N. Galpern, *The*

Religions of the People in 16th Century Champagne (Princeton, 1981); John McManners, *Death and the Enlightenment* (Oxford, 1981); Christina Larner, *Enemies of God* (Baltimore, 1981); and Timothy Tackett, *Priest and Parish in 18th Century France* (Princeton, 1977).

Specifically concerned with popular culture are Peter Burke, *Popular Culture in Early Modern Europe* (London, 1978), a good introduction to the subject, with bibliography; Alan Dundes and Alessandro Falassi, *La Terra in Piazza* (Berkeley, 1975), in English, on the *palio* of Siena; Carlo Ginzburg, *The Cheese and the Worms* (Baltimore, 1980); and Jean Claude Schmitt, *The Holy Greyhound* (N.Y., 1983).

On the question of literacy, see Jack Goody, ed., *Literacy in Traditional Societies* (Cambridge, 1968); and Harvey Graff, ed., *Literacy and Social Development in the West* (Cambridge, 1981). On the history of women, a good bibliographical orientation is to be found in Joan Scott and Olwen Hufton, "Women in History," *Past and Present* (November, 1983), 125–157.

INDEX

Absentee owners: of Sennely, 1–3; resentment of by impoverished peasants, 78–79

Alt-Limpurg Society: fellowship of the *Geschlechter,* 46; peasant background, 78

Aristocracy: narrow élite, 59–60. *See also* Privileged estates; Nobility

Associations: in response to isolation, 107–110. *See also* Craft fellowships

Azereix: impoverishment resulting from tax burden, 76–77

Barefoot Men of Normandy (Avranches): peasant rebellion of 1639, 82; reaction against salt tax, 87

Beauvais: illustrative of the seventeenth-century commune, 24–28; and impoverished nobles, 58–59

Beggars: as marginal members of communities, 102–103

Bennassar, Bartolomé: study of Valladolid, 48

Black Death: effects on fifteenth-century peasants, 74; cause of labor shortage, 113

Bordeaux: revolt of 1651, 99–100

Bouchard, Gérard: study of Sennely, 1; *Le village immobile,* 10

Bourgeois: concept of communal membership, 21; distinguished from commune inhabitants, 22; as perceived by nobles, 23; oligarchy in Beauvais, 26; free peasants, 69

Brittany: prosperity of the new urban élite, 61

Bubonic plague: from 1347 to 1721, 11–12. *See also* Black Death

Bürger (native-born citizens) of Frankfurt: 44–46

Caballeros (gentlemen): urban élite in Valladolid, 48

Calvinists: lack of integration in Frankfurt, 44–45

Carnival in Romans (Emmanuel Le Roy Ladurie). *See* Dauphiné rebellion

Carnival of St. Blaise's feast: role in the Dauphiné rebellion, 93, 97

Censos (private *rentes*): and *rentier* wealth, 48

Châteaudouble: 1597 assault on, 94–95

Child transporters: shipping of orphans to foundling hospitals, 103–104

Children: of Sennely, 2; socialization of in Siena, 36–37; of indigent laborers, 103; abandoned by slave mothers, 115. *See also* Orphans

Christian Europe: population in fourteenth century, 10; in the thirteenth century, 19–20

Cities: medieval, 14–29; crime and security in, 16–17; and total urban population, 17; European distinguished from others, 18–19; growth during twelfth century, 19; population in the sixteenth century, 20; development of Craft fellowships during medieval period, 24; independence from constraints, 30; daily schedule, 35; loss of autonomy after the sixteenth century, 55

Citizenship: without trade or Craft membership, 43–46; and traveling journeymen, 112; requirements for, 154*n*

Clergy: as a privileged estate, 56; suspicions of public schools, 134–135; peasant resentment of, 142–143; medieval roots of antagonism with laity, 147–149

Cloth trade: in Beauvais, 25–27

Colas, Jacques: in the Dauphiné rebellion, 90–100

GEORGE HUPPERT, Professor of History at the University of Illinois at Chicago, is the author of *The Idea of Perfect History*, *Les Bourgeois Gentilshommes: An Essay on the Definition of Elites in Renaissance France*, and *Public Schools in Renaissance France*, as well as numerous essays and articles on the social history of early modern Europe.